6484

DATE DUE

MAY 18 1994			
FEB 08 1991			
MAR 0 5 1995			

AMERICA the BEAUTIFUL

IDAHO

By Zachary Kent

Consultants

Gordon Murri, Director of Curriculum and Instructional Materials, Pocatello Public Schools

R. B. Reddington, Author, *Horizons of Idaho*

Robert L. Hillerich, Ph.D., Bowling Green State University, Bowling Green, Ohio

CHILDRENS PRESS ®

CHICAGO

Isabella Creek in Clearwater National Forest

Project Editor: Joan Downing
Associate Editor: Shari Joffe
Design Director: Margrit Fiddle
Typesetting: Graphic Connections, Inc.
Engraving: Liberty Photoengraving

Library of Congress Cataloging-in-Publication Data

Kent, Zachary.
  America the beautiful. Idaho / by Zachary Kent.
    p.   cm.
  Includes index.
  Summary: Introduces the geography, history,
government, economy, industry, culture, historic
sites, and famous people of the Gem State.
    ISBN 0-516-00458-1
    1. Idaho—Juvenile literature. [1. Idaho.]
I. Title.
F746.3.K46   1990
979.6—dc20   89-25280
                                                CIP
                                                AC

Old and new juxtaposed in downtown Boise

TABLE OF CONTENTS

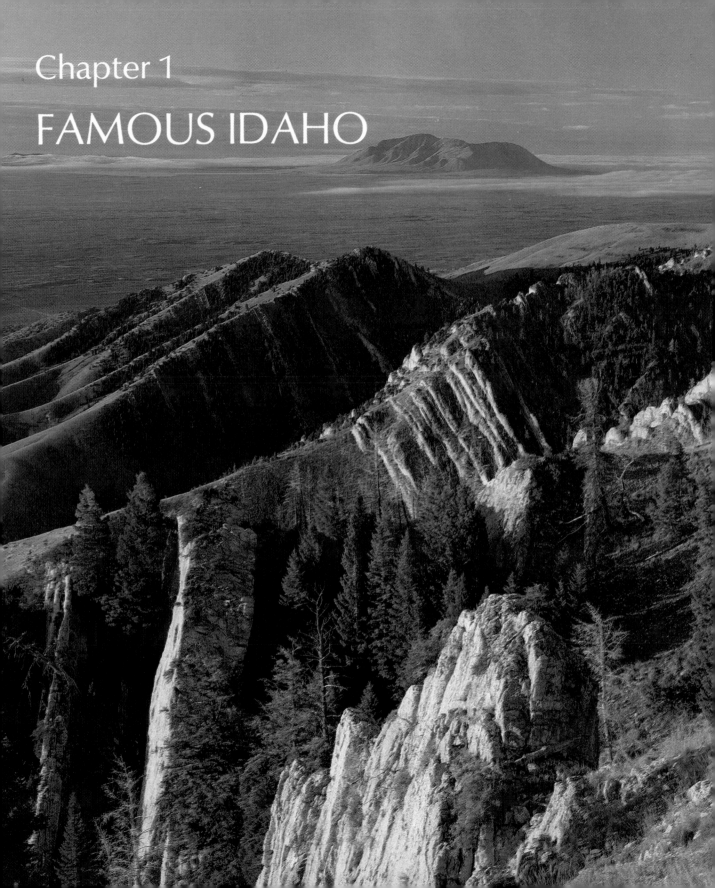

Chapter 1

FAMOUS IDAHO

FAMOUS IDAHO

Mention the state of Idaho anywhere in the United States and the response will likely be, "Oh yes, Idaho potatoes." For decades, Idaho has been America's leading producer of potatoes. Chances are that each time you order french fries in a fast-food restaurant or cut into a steaming baked potato at your family dinner table, you are eating something that has come from Idaho.

To many, the words *Idaho* and *potatoes* seem inseparable. It is no surprise to find the slogan "Famous Potatoes" stamped on Idaho's automobile license plates. Yet the successful farming of potatoes reveals only a small fraction of Idaho's fascinating story.

A rugged and beautiful state, Idaho is a land of spectacular variety and brilliant contrasts. The last American state to be visited by white civilization, Idaho has abundant natural resources and breathtaking scenery that have attracted settlers ever since.

Through the years, Idaho's farmers, miners, lumbermen, and manufacturers have fought to make the land their own. Their proud heritage is full of deeds that reflect the hardships of conquering a wilderness. Snowcapped mountains, rocky river gorges, lush forests, and vast deserts are all a part of Idaho. In the end, it is the state's ability to hold the past intact while reaching out to touch the future that brings Idaho its greatest fame.

Chapter 2
THE LAND

THE LAND

*On descending the heights of the mountains the soil
becomes gradually more fertile, and the land through
which we passed this evening, is of excellent quality.*
— from the journals of Lewis and Clark, 1805

*The country all the way down the Snake River is one of the
most desolate and dreary wastes in the world. Light, soft
ground with no soil on top, looking like an ash heap . . .*
— settler E. S. McComas in 1862

GEOGRAPHY AND TOPOGRAPHY

The varied lands that make up Idaho are both enchanting and
forbidding. On a map, the shape of the state roughly resembles the
letter *L*. Covering an area of 83,564 square miles (216,431 square
kilometers), Idaho ranks thirteenth in size among the fifty states.
From north to south, the state stretches 483 miles (777
kilometers). Idaho's greatest east-west distance, along the state's
southern border, is 316 miles (509 kilometers). However, the
northernmost part of the state measures only about 45 miles
(72 kilometers) from east to west. Within these unusual
boundaries lie land formations of truly dramatic proportion and
scope.

Over millions of years, the continuous upheaval of the earth
shaped the surface of Idaho. Rumbling earthquakes thrust
mountains skyward. Huge volcanic eruptions poured lava and
sent clouds of volcanic ash to layer the ground. The incredible

The magnificent Sawtooth Mountains of south-central Idaho

weight of glacial ice packs battered the land and tore deep valleys
between the mountains. About thirty thousand years ago, glacial
ice formed vast Bonneville Lake, which covered parts of Idaho,
Wyoming, and Utah. When it suddenly overflowed, the resulting
"Bonneville Flood" ripped through southern Idaho. About twenty
thousand years ago, a great cork of ice burst in northern Idaho,
unleashing another gigantic glacial lake. Called the "Spokane
Flood," these surging waters left behind lasting valleys and lakes.

The name *Idaho* was invented in 1860 by a lobbyist named
George Willing. Originally wanting the name to be used for the
territory that was to become Colorado, Willing told Congress that
it meant "gem of the mountains" in an Indian language. Even
though it was soon revealed that the word had been invented, it
was eventually used for the territory that became present-day
Idaho. Indeed, of all of the state's land features, its snow-covered

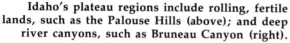
Idaho's plateau regions include rolling, fertile lands, such as the Palouse Hills (above); and deep river canyons, such as Bruneau Canyon (right).

mountains are the most striking. Among the hundreds of mountains in Idaho, forty-two rise more than 10,000 feet (3,048 meters). Towering Borah Peak, part of the spectacular Lost River Range, is the tallest mountain, at 12,662 feet (3,859 meters). In this land of snowy ridges, it is not surprising that the state's average elevation is over 5,000 feet (1,524 meters).

The Selkirk Mountains dominate the Idaho "Panhandle," the narrow, northernmost part of Idaho. Just to the south are the mineral-rich Coeur d'Alene Mountains. These are part of the vast Bitterroot Range, which spreads southward and forms a natural border between Idaho and Montana. Among the more than twenty other ranges in Idaho are the Clearwater, Salmon River, Sawtooth, Boise, and Caribou mountains. They all are part of the great Rocky Mountains, which span western North America from Alaska to New Mexico.

Beside the foothills of Idaho's mountains lie high, broad
plateaus. Deep river canyons cut through some of these prairie
lands. Where the land rolls undisturbed, however, rich topsoil
deposits make farming possible. The Palouse Hills of the
Clearwater Plateau, for example, sway with the golden beauty of
fine wheat crops year after year.

In striking contrast, prehistoric lava beds and sagebrush-
strangled deserts still cover much of the plateau lands of the great
Snake River Plain. The Snake River Plain sweeps across southern
Idaho in a huge arc that is hundreds of miles wide. Each evening,
the setting sun paints the rough landscape with fabulous colors
and eerie shadows.

RIVERS AND LAKES

Idaho boasts more than 16,000 miles (25,749 kilometers) of
rivers and streams. The Bear River, which empties into Utah's
Great Salt Lake, is the state's only southeastward-flowing river.

The rest flow westward, feeding into the Columbia River before reaching the Pacific Ocean. The greatest of these is the Snake River, referred to by the Shoshone Indians as the "River of the Sagebrush Plain." Born in the mountains of Wyoming's Yellowstone National Park, the Snake River twists and turns on its 1,000-mile (1,609-kilometer) journey across Idaho. Along its winding course, the Snake crashes over misty waterfalls and tears through rocky canyons.

Two major rivers flow entirely within Idaho. The wild Salmon River has come to be known as the "River of No Return." Its waters flow with such intensity that only the most expert guides dare lead thrill-packed rafting expeditions downstream. Against its raging currents, only jet-powered boats can successfully travel upstream. Much more inviting is the Clearwater River. At different times in Idaho's history, the Clearwater River was used by explorers, miners, and loggers. Today, people who love to fish cast their lines along the Clearwater with wonderful results, and vacationing campers pitch their tents beside its banks.

Many of the state's other beautiful rivers attract visitors as well. The St. Joe, St. Maries, and Coeur d'Alene, for example, all provided important routes during Idaho's river-logging heyday. In the north, the Kootenai, Pend Oreille, and Spokane all eventually feed into the Columbia River in the state of Washington. Farther south, two unusual rivers flow out of the Lost River Range. The Big Lost River and the Little Lost River both end in Butte County, where they simply sink and disappear beneath ancient lava formations.

Eleven man-made dams block the natural progress of the Snake River. These dams and those on other Idaho rivers provide essential waterpower and create huge reservoirs. The largest of the state's artificial lakes is the American Falls Reservoir, which

Shoshone Falls (left) and Payette Lake (right)

lies in three counties. Palisades, Blackfoot River, Anderson Ranch, Lucky Peak, Cascade, and Dworshak reservoirs all offer Idahoans fabulous recreational opportunities.

Sports enthusiasts and vacationers need not depend on Idaho's man-made lakes for fun, however. More than two thousand natural lakes also grace Idaho's landscape. The largest of these is Lake Pend Oreille, which covers 148 square miles (383 square kilometers) in the Panhandle region. Also in northern Idaho are the sparkling, broad waters and tree-lined shores of Priest Lake, Hayden Lake, and Coeur d'Alene Lake. Perhaps even more beautiful is snow-fed Payette Lake, near McCall in the central part of the state. Lovely Henry's Lake, near the Wyoming border, and Bear Lake, which lies in the southeast corner of the state and extends into Utah, are also popular recreational lakes.

CLIMATE

Throughout the year, Idahoans experience a wide variety of weather conditions. Winter snows in the high mountains sometimes exceed an annual rate of 200 inches (508 centimeters). When the snow melts in summer, it feeds the state's many lakes and streams. Generally, northern Idaho receives about 32 inches (81 centimeters) of rain and snowfall a year. The Snake River Plain to the south, however, seldom enjoys more than 10 inches (25 centimeters) of precipitation annually.

Visitors to Idaho in the summer and fall generally find the climate warm and delightful. Hot, rainless weather, though, sometimes creates special dangers for Idahoans, as dry timber can easily burst into flame when sparked by lightning. Devastating forest fires occurred in the state in 1910, 1919, and 1934. "The number of large fires has just been overwhelming," declared Idaho forest-fire specialist Marvin F. Newell in 1986. That year, summer blazes north of Boise charred an area the size of the state of Rhode Island. In 1988, forest fires throughout the western states raged even more fiercely. By the time September showers arrived to ease the threat, more than 300,000 acres (121,407 hectares) of Idaho's forests had been scorched.

Temperatures across Idaho vary widely. Warm, moist air blows east from the Pacific Ocean, keeping the Idaho Panhandle seasonably comfortable. Also, the mountains along the eastern border of Idaho tend to hold back cold winter winds from the north and east. However, frigid temperatures can occur in the mountainous areas. On January 18, 1943, the temperature at Island Park Dam dropped to minus 60 degrees Fahrenheit (minus 51 degrees Celsius), the coldest temperature ever recorded in Idaho. On July 28, 1934, Orofino experienced a sweltering all-time

Aspens (left) and Indian paintbrush (right) brighten Idaho's landscape.

high of 118 degrees Fahrenheit (48 degrees Celsius). Summers are comfortably warm throughout most of Idaho.

PLANTS AND WILDLIFE

Fully 40 percent of Idaho is covered by forest. Although logging operations and fires have claimed their share, the abundance and variety of Idaho's trees remains astonishing. Several kinds of pines, Douglas firs, spruces, and western larches stand thick and green on the mountainsides. Beside valley streams, the leafy branches of birches, willows, and aspens tremble with every breeze. Western hemlocks grow in hardy groves. Some of the state's stands of red cedar date back several hundred years.

Idaho's mountain forests shelter all kinds of animals. Beneath snowberry and chokecherry bushes, chipmunks and squirrels dig

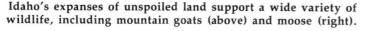
Idaho's expanses of unspoiled land support a wide variety of wildlife, including mountain goats (above) and moose (right).

among the pine needles. Porcupines and beavers gnaw on bark for nourishment. Moose, elk, and white-tailed deer nibble the tender buds of shrubs or graze on meadow grasses. Lynxes, cougars, and wolverines creep stealthily among the trees before pouncing on unwary prey. With sharp-clawed paws, black bears and grizzly bears snag fish from alpine streams and lakes. Some animals thrive in the cold heights above the timberline. Mountain goats munch on mosses along rocky ledges, while pikas—small rabbitlike rodents—find grassy nooks in which to nest.

In the early 1800s, millions of buffalo roamed across the grasslands of Idaho's plateaus. For many years, however, they were thoughtlessly slaughtered by man, and today, less than two thousand of the great shaggy beasts remain in Idaho. Yet other wildlife still abounds here. Deer mice, prairie dogs, and badgers all burrow in the soil. Pronghorn antelopes and bighorn sheep can be found among the hills. Waving fields of wheatgrass, fescue, and the white-flowered shrub syringa (the state flower) give way to

The Snake River Birds of Prey Natural Area is the home of the world's largest concentration of nesting hawks (above), eagles, and prairie falcons.

sagebrush, rabbitbrush, greasewood, and cheatgrass in the southern Idaho desert. Rodents such as voles and marmots live on this dry terrain, as do horned toads, rattlesnakes, and whiptailed lizards. Jackrabbits chased by bobcats race amidst the sagebrush, while coyotes howl beneath the moonlit sky.

Bird-watchers rarely leave Idaho dissatisfied. More than 360 different species have been spotted in the state. They range in size from the tiny calliope hummingbird to the great blue heron. Their colors vary from the vivid blue of the mountain bluebird (the state bird) to the startling red, yellow, and black feathers of the western tanager. Across the glassy surface of Idaho's lakes, Canada geese, mallards, and trumpeter swans glide gracefully. Such game birds as ring-necked pheasants, mourning doves, quails, grouse, and chukar and Hungarian partridges can be found in many areas. From the rocky cliffs overlooking the Snake River, such birds of prey as the golden eagle, red-tailed hawk, and prairie falcon swoop and swirl on airy currents.

Chapter 3
THE
PEOPLE

THE PEOPLE

Along U.S. Highway 95 just north of Lucile, a monument stands
in memory of Dr. Wilson A. Foskett. For twenty-seven years,
Dr. Foskett faithfully served the people of western Idaho County,
setting bones, pulling aching teeth, and delivering babies. When,
in 1924, Doc Foskett died tragically in a car accident after working
late one night, his stunned friends and patients decided to honor
him with a monument.

Boise music-store owner Charlie Sampson touched the hearts of
a number of Idahoans as well. The cheerful salesman often
crisscrossed the state making deliveries. In 1914, as a service to the
public, he started painting arrows along nineteen unmarked
routes leading to Boise. Soon, the "Sampson Trails" became
famous as amusing and valuable Idaho travelers' aids. "Yes, we'll
miss Charlie Sampson," declared the *Idaho Statesman* after his
death in 1935.

In recent years, people living in the remote Salmon River
Mountains have depended on the Arnold Aviation Service, based
in Cascade. Over her shortwave radio, Carol Arnold receives
shopping lists from backwoods customers. Then, as often as twice
a week in good weather, her husband flies in the mail and the
supplies. The approaching sound of Ray Arnold's small plane
always brings grateful friends hurrying from their isolated
mountain cabins.

Although Idahoans generally value their sense of independence,
they also share deep feelings of community. In a vast state where

21

geography often spreads people apart, Idahoans try to find ways to draw together and help each other.

POPULATION

According to the 1980 census, Idaho has a population of 944,038. An estimate in 1987 placed Idaho's population at 1,003,000. Among the fifty states, Idaho ranks forty-first in number of people.

In recent years, Idaho's natural beauty and growing business opportunities have been drawing more and more people from other states. Projections suggest that by the year 2000, more than 1.5 million people will call themselves Idahoans. Since Idaho's population density is only 11 people per square mile (4 people per square kilometer), the state has plenty of room for new citizens.

Two of every three Idahoans live in the Snake River Valley in the southern part of the state. Huge irrigation projects there have transformed sagebrush desert into fertile farmland. As a result, the state's biggest cities thrive in that region. The capital city of Boise, which lies on the Boise River, is by far the largest city, with a population of 102,160. Pocatello, Idaho Falls, Twin Falls, and Nampa are other lively southern cities. Idaho's largest northern cities are Lewiston, which grew up where the Snake and the Clearwater rivers meet; and Coeur d'Alene, which lies across the border from Spokane, Washington. Fully 60 percent of Idaho's citizens live in urban areas.

ETHNIC IDAHO

The overwhelming majority of Idahoans are white, native-born Americans of European ancestry. Idaho's foreign-born population

The Shoshone-Bannock Indian Festival is held each August at the Fort Hall Indian Reservation.

is small but growing. Recently, opportunities in agriculture and industry have been attracting Mexicans and Asians.

In the practice of religion, most follow one of the Protestant faiths. The Lutheran, Presbyterian, Baptist, and Methodist churches are among the Protestant denominations represented in Idaho. The Church of Jesus Christ of Latter-day Saints (also known as the Mormon church) has a sizable following in the state. Roman Catholics have worshipped in Idaho since the 1830s.

Among those who have lived in the state for generations are many ethnic groups with rich cultural heritages. More than ten thousand Native Americans (American Indians) live on the state's four reservations. Finns and Swedes migrated to Idaho in the late 1800s to cut timber for the logging industry and plow farms in the Panhandle. Around the same time, some black railroad workers stayed after laying tracks in southern Idaho. Today, most of Idaho's twenty-seven hundred blacks are concentrated in Boise and Pocatello. In the 1890s, Italian immigrants helped build the Great Northern Railroad through Idaho. Afterward, they settled in such towns as Priest River and Naples.

Two other ethnic groups have made an impact upon the state:
Chinese and Basques. The excitement of Idaho's 1860s gold rush
first brought Chinese to the region. Their long braided hair,
strange clothes, and foreign customs made some white miners
uneasy, and they were often treated poorly. Still, the Chinese
eagerly worked worn-out mines that other laborers would no
longer touch. By 1870, more than four thousand Chinese lived in
Idaho, making up nearly one-third of the territory's population at
that time. When the gold-rush days ended, many Chinese
pioneers stayed to run restaurants, businesses, and farms.

People of the Basque region of northern Spain found their way
to Idaho in the 1800s. Many came from sheepherding families,
and Idaho sheep ranchers gladly hired the Basques to tend their
flocks. The Basque sheepherders learned quickly and prospered. In
time, stories of success and opportunity brought other Basques
from Spain. Today, the rich Basque culture is still evident in the
Boise Valley. At festivals and on religious holidays, people of
Basque ancestry gather to sing the Basque anthem ("Guerniks'ko
Arbola"), dance the jota in traditional folk costumes, and toss the
palanka (javelin).

REGIONALISM

In Idaho, mountain ranges and desert lands are natural barriers that divide the state. It is not surprising, then, that a deep sense of regionalism is felt in various sections of the state. People in northern Idaho raged in 1864 when the territorial legislature voted to move the capital from Lewiston to the larger city of Boise. The northern Idahoans felt insulted and ignored by the south. Lewiston citizens placed the territory's seals and documents under a twenty-four-hour guard. In April 1865, territorial secretary C. DeWitt Smith stole them and carried them off to Boise. Some northern Idahoans still complain that their rightful capital was stolen from them.

Through the years, northern Idahoans have looked west to the nearby commercial and transportation centers of Washington State rather than south to Boise. Even today, only one major road—U.S. Highway 95—winds through the mountains to link the northern and southern parts of Idaho, and that road was not even paved until 1938.

Religion has created a sense of regionalism in southeastern Idaho. Originally settled by Mormons, the area is still dominated by that religious group. The close-knit ways of the Mormons helped them survive through many difficult years. The church remains the core of many Mormons' lives, and Mormons often look south to Salt Lake City, the center of Mormonism, for business opportunities and guidance.

The differences in outlook and customs that exist within Idaho are part of what makes the state so interesting. All of the state's citizens, whether they live in the north, the southeast, or the Boise Basin, are ultimately united by their pride in and concern for Idaho.

25

Chapter 4
THE BEGINNING

THE BEGINNING

THE FIRST IDAHOANS

In 1960, archaeologists digging in Wilson Butte Cave in southern Idaho's Jerome County made some startling discoveries. Shards of rough pottery, notched arrowheads, and even a leather moccasin offered evidence of Idaho's earliest inhabitants. Scientific radiocarbon dating revealed that these artifacts were over 13,500 years old.

The first people to live in Idaho left remnants of their cultures in other places as well. Pictographs (designs painted on rocks) and petroglyphs (symbols scratched into rocks) survive today in the Coeur d'Alene Lake, Lake Pend Oreille, and Priest Lake regions of the state, as well as along the Salmon and Snake rivers. Although this rock art proves that people roamed Idaho thousands of years ago, the meaning of their strange messages continues to baffle archaeologists.

Gradually, several Native American groups settled in the Idaho region. The Kootenai, Pend d'Oreille, and Coeur d'Alene groups ranged through the north. In the mountains of the central region, the Nez Perce group took hold. Farther south, the Shoshone and the related Bannock groups made the plains of the Snake River Valley their home. The northern Paiute roamed across southwestern Idaho.

Through the centuries, Idaho's Indians thrived on nature's bounty. In the forests and across the prairies, the men stalked

The Appaloosa, a sturdy breed of horse, was developed centuries ago by the Nez Perce.

deer, elk, and bear, which they killed with bows and arrows. On mountain lakes and along valley streams, they speared and netted trout and salmon. They also hunted ducks, geese, rabbits, and other prey. The women gathered berries, nuts, and wild plants to eat. Many of the Indians considered *camas* a vital part of their diets. At harvesttime, the women used pointed sticks to dig up the bulbs of these blue flowers. Crushed and pounded into cakes, camas fed the people during the snowbound winter months.

THE COMING OF THE HORSE

At the start of the 1500s, European explorers began to claim portions of North America for their kings and queens. Another two hundred years would pass, however, before European culture would first touch the lives of Idaho's natives. From Spanish outposts in New Mexico, local Indians learned of the horse and spread its usage northward. Sometime after 1730, the Shoshone

Indians saw the wondrous beast for the first time. They acquired horses for themselves, and the animal soon changed their way of life. Across the prairies, skilled Shoshone hunters galloped after herds of buffalo. As the herds wandered east and west, nomadic Indian bands now followed after them.

Many Idaho Indians considered horses their most important possessions. The Nez Perce became renowned as expert horse breeders. In the hilly Palouse region, they developed an especially sturdy, surefooted breed. Easily recognized by its mix of spots and solid coloring, the Appaloosa breed is today known throughout the world. Unfortunately, horses were not the only "gift" brought to North America by the Europeans. Through the years, smallpox and other European diseases swept through Idaho, killing thousands of defenseless Native Americans.

LEWIS AND CLARK

"Tab-ba-bone!" That word, thought to mean "white man" in the Shoshone language, echoed through the Idaho mountains in the summer of 1805. In 1803, the United States purchased the vast Louisiana territory from France. The next year, President Thomas Jefferson sent Captains Meriwether Lewis and William Clark up the Missouri River on a heroic expedition into this unexplored new region. Wanting to strengthen American claims to the disputed Oregon territory beyond the Rocky Mountains, Jefferson hoped Lewis and Clark's "Corps of Discovery" would cut a path all the way to the Pacific Ocean.

On August 12, 1805, Captain Lewis ventured through Lemhi Pass and noticed that a nearby creek flowed westward instead of eastward. Instantly he realized that at long last, he had crossed the Continental Divide. He knelt down at this stream that would

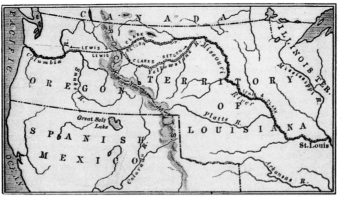

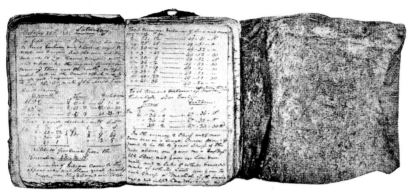

eventually empty into the Columbia River, and as he later wrote in his journal, "Here I first tasted the water of the great Columbia River." Lewis and his excited scouts became the first white people to set foot in present-day Idaho.

Natives of the Lemhi band of the Shoshone soon welcomed the white explorers into their villages. Traveling with Lewis and Clark was a young Indian woman named Sacagawea. Sacagawea was a Shoshone, but had been captured by enemy Indians and taken east in 1800. As an interpreter, she had already proven her worth to the Corps of Discovery many times. Now seated at the council to translate for Lewis and Clark, Sacagawea cried out in surprise. Cameahwait, the Lemhi chief, she realized tearfully, was her own brother.

Gladly, the Lemhi Shoshone agreed to help the white explorers journey westward. Farther to the north, the party hiked through

Lolo Pass into the forbidding Bitterroot Mountains. Many weeks of hard travel lay ahead. Reaching the Clearwater and the Snake rivers, the expedition forged onward. As the explorers passed among the Nez Perce Indians, the presence of Sacagawea and her baby son calmed fears that the whites were anything but peaceful. Two months' travel carried the Corps of Discovery out of the Idaho region. After successfully reaching the Columbia River and the Pacific Ocean, the expedition journeyed again through Idaho along the Lolo Trail on their long trip back home. Lewis and Clark had discovered that the terrain of Idaho offered a difficult gateway to the Pacific and a wealth of unknown opportunities.

THE FUR COMPANIES

In the early 1800s, gentlemen of fashion strolled the streets of Europe wearing tall, elegant fur hats. This sudden trend had made beaver skins very valuable. Soon after Lewis and Clark departed the Idaho wilderness, adventurous trappers cut new paths in search of furs. Well-established British trading companies, such as the Hudson's Bay Company and the rival North West Company, made the earliest claims upon the region. From Canada, hardy company trappers edged southward. Along Idaho's swirling streams they set their traps. Leading the way in 1808, David Thompson arrived to explore the region for the North West Company. In 1809, Thompson hefted an ax and built Kullyspell House on the eastern shore of Lake Pend Oreille. This temporary trading post was the first white establishment in Idaho. Here and elsewhere, the British welcomed the Indians. Eagerly they exchanged guns, knives, pots, and mirrors for stacks of lustrous beaver pelts.

Ambitious Americans also competed for Idaho furs. Andrew

Henry, a partner in the St. Louis Fur Company, led nearly four hundred trappers into southeastern Idaho in 1810. In present-day Fremont County, they built Fort Henry. Winter hunger forced these men to eat their horses, however. In the spring of 1811, the party abandoned the site.

Undaunted by the hardships of the wilderness, wealthy New Yorker John Jacob Astor hoped to expand his fur-trading empire throughout the Pacific Northwest. In 1811, Astor sent a fearless, sixty-three member expedition west from St. Louis. These "Astorians," commanded by Wilson Price Hunt, were to lay claims to the Idaho region while traveling to Fort Astoria at the mouth of the Columbia River in Oregon. Troubles plagued Hunt's party throughout their journey. The cruel rapids of the uncharted Snake River wrecked canoes and drowned one man in a rocky canyon that the Astorians dubbed "Cauldron Linn." The party hiked overland for the last 800 miles (1,287 kilometers), during which freezing winter weather claimed more lives. The return trip in 1812 proved equally difficult. Again the pioneers had learned the harsh cost Idaho demanded for its natural riches.

THE MOUNTAIN MEN

Fur trappers called the giant Scotsman "Perpetual Motion" because of his constant energy, and "King of the Northwest" because of his leadership. Standing six feet, four inches tall and weighing three hundred pounds, veteran explorer Donald MacKenzie of the North West Company reentered Idaho from Washington in 1818. For three years, MacKenzie led into Idaho daring Scots, French Canadian *voyageurs* (men employed by a fur company to transport goods and men to and from remote locations), and Iroquois Indian trappers in search of beaver.

The rugged fur trappers and traders of the Northwest were known as mountain men.

MacKenzie's "Snake River Brigades" broke into small groups as they pushed eastward. They explored the Snake River and all of the streams that flowed into it. At promising spots, these mountain men waded into the icy water and staked their traps. They carefully rubbed castoreum, a substance taken from a gland in beavers, on nearby twigs. The musky odor of castoreum attracted prey. A successful capture was signaled by the snap of a trap's steel jaws. Skinned and stretched on a willow hoop, a prime beaver hide could fetch as much as six dollars—a hefty sum of money in those days.

A Hudson's Bay Company trading post

British expeditions such as MacKenzie's and those that followed after him trapped out many of Idaho's rivers during the 1820s. American mountain men, however, refused to surrender the region to the British. Journeying through Wyoming's Teton Mountains, several hundred American trappers fanned out for miles across eastern Idaho.

RENDEZVOUS AND TRADING POSTS

To collect furs and to keep their far-flung trappers supplied, the owners of the Rocky Mountain Fur Company devised a system of yearly rendezvous (meetings at an appointed place and time). In 1826 and 1827, for example, trappers gathered at Bear Lake in the Cache Valley. In 1832, the largest trapper rendezvous ever held met at Pierre's Hole in present-day Teton County, "the best valley in the world," according to famed mountain man Jim Bridger. For one week in July, hundreds of buckskinned trappers and friendly Indians set up camp, traded furs, swapped stories, and competed in frontier sports.

When Boston trader Nathaniel Wyeth arrived at the 1834 rendezvous, he discovered that most of the Idaho mountain men

A reconstruction of Fort Hall

had already purchased their supplies. In order to sell his goods, Wyeth put his men to work constructing a permanent outlet. "I have built a fort on Snake . . . river which I named Fort Hall," he wrote. "Its bastions stand a terror to the skulking Indians and a beacon of safety to the fugitive hunter." To compete with this fortified trading post, the British Hudson's Bay Company soon established Fort Boise at the mouth of the Boise River near the site of present-day Parma.

THE FIRST MISSIONARIES

During rare visits to Fort Hall and Fort Boise, the trappers made contact with the outside world. In the wilderness, however, these free-spirited adventurers lived more like Indians than white men. Generally, the two cultures mingled in peace. As early as 1831, two Nez Perce Indians, Rabbit Skin Leggings and No Horns on His Head, journeyed to St. Louis as messengers. After their visit, a myth developed that the Indians wanted the Christian religion brought to their people, and several missionaries responded.

A nineteenth-century photograph of a missionary among a group of
Nez Perce women at Lapwai

Jason Lee, a Methodist minister from New England, traveled
west with Nathaniel Wyeth's supply caravan in 1834. At Fort
Hall, he performed the region's first Sunday service before
pushing on to Oregon. Other missionaries followed. In 1836,
Marcus and Narcissa Whitman and Henry and Eliza Spalding
ventured together into the Pacific Northwest. Narcissa and Eliza
became the first white women to cross the continent. The
Whitmans established a mission near present-day Walla Walla,
Washington, while the Spaldings built a small mission house at
Lapwai Creek, just east of present-day Lewiston. With energy,
Henry Spalding erected Idaho's first sawmill and gristmill. He
planted the region's first orchard and encouraged the Nez Perce to
learn farming methods. At the Spalding mission school, Eliza
tirelessly drew pictures and used interpreters to teach stories from

The Cataldo Mission, built in 1850 by Coeur d'Alene Indians under the direction of Jesuit priests, is Idaho's oldest standing building.

the Bible. Dozens of Nez Perce crowded into the school to learn about Christianity. The Spaldings remained active in Idaho until 1847. That year, a massacre at the Whitman's mission by enraged Cayuse Indians forced the Spaldings to flee for safety.

Roman Catholics of the Jesuit order brought their religion to Idaho as well. Coeur d'Alene Indians welcomed Father Pierre-Jean De Smet in late 1842. At De Smet's Mission of the Sacred Heart beside the St. Joe River, Indians gathered to learn the rituals of the Roman Catholic faith. In 1846, Father Joseph Hoset shifted the mission's site to a hill overlooking the Coeur d'Alene River. In 1850, Father Anthony Ravalli started construction of a lasting mission there. With simple tools, the Indians joined in the effort. Axmen hewed round logs into square beams. Using drawknives, workers fashioned planks for flooring. Wooden pegs locked every timber into place. The outer walls were carefully daubed with mud. After three years of labor, the priests and Indians admired the finished Coeur d'Alene Mission. Named the Cataldo Mission in honor of mission priest Father Joseph Cataldo, the mission today remains the oldest building still standing in Idaho.

THE OREGON TRAIL

As early as the 1830s, stories of the fertile Oregon country lured Americans westward. Following paths beaten by Idaho's fur trappers, small parties of settlers plodded for miles across the dry and dangerous countryside. Stops at trading posts for water and food supplies were crucial. In 1839, a weary traveler remembered gratefully reaching Fort Boise: "... we were Received ... in a very polite and genteel manner and entertained Sumtuously by our Host ... our table was furnished with ... fowls, Ducks, Bacon, Salmon, Sturgeon, Buffalow, & Elk. ..." Captain Benjamin Bonneville had first proved that wagons could be brought across the Rocky Mountains during his western explorations in the 1830s. In 1841, the creaking wheels of the first Oregon-bound wagon train could be heard crossing the Idaho territory.

In 1843, the United States Army asked John C. Frémont to map and survey the best trail to Oregon. With mountain men Kit Carson and Thomas Fitzpatrick as his guides, Frémont crisscrossed southern Idaho. His maps and reports of the region won him the nickname "The Pathfinder" and convinced more Americans to pack their possessions and journey west. In ox-drawn covered wagons called "prairie schooners," travelers loaded tools, furniture, and sacks of flour, salt, sugar, and seeds for planting. Pioneers began the great 2,000-mile (3,219-kilometer) trek at Independence, Missouri. At South Pass, with

A replica of a prairie schooner at Three Island Crossing State Park, once an important site along the Oregon Trail

hundreds of miles still to go, they entered Idaho. Graves marked with crude wooden crosses beside the trail in Idaho told sad tales of freezing snowstorms, starvation, sickness, and Indian attacks along the way.

In spite of hardship, the flow of hopeful emigrants continued. Some one thousand settlers passed through Idaho in 1843. By 1850, the wagons of about fifty-five thousand travelers had deepened the dusty ruts of the Oregon Trail. The discovery of gold in California in 1848 increased traffic along the road. At Hudspeth's Cutoff near Soda Springs, and again at Fort Hall, thousands of excited miners stampeded south along trails leading to California.

Both the beautiful farmlands of Oregon and the goldfields of California brought Americans through Idaho. But the rugged region itself seemingly offered no attractions to entice settlers to stay. South Idaho seemed too dry to encourage settlement. In fact, as silk hats replaced fur hats as fashionable headwear, many mountain men left Idaho to find their fortunes elsewhere. It would take another generation of Americans to lay permanent claim to Idaho.

Chapter 5
PIONEER DAYS

PIONEER DAYS

Great Britain at last gave up its claim to the lands south of the 49th parallel (today's United States-Canada border) in 1846. Though Idaho was at first considered part of the vast Oregon Territory, in time, Idaho's pioneers established a separate identity for their region.

THE MORMONS

The Church of Jesus Christ of Latter-day Saints was first established by Joseph Smith in New York in 1830. Its followers, commonly called Mormons, sought to practice their new faith in peace. Many people, however, disapproved of the Mormons' belief that a man should be allowed to have more than one wife at a time. Hounded as he and his followers moved from place to place, church president Brigham Young at last decided to lead the persecuted Mormons to the "promised land." Starting in 1846, thousands of Mormons journeyed west across the plains and desert. At Salt Lake City in present-day Utah, they founded their new Mormon center.

To take a firmer hold of the region, Young urged his followers to spread out and colonize. The devout band of missionaries who trekked 380 miles (612 kilometers) north into Idaho in 1855 hoped to convert the Bannock and Shoshone Indians they encountered. The ringing sound of axes chopping wood brought many curious Indians to the site of the first Mormon mission. "Our fort stands on the eastern bank of the Limhi River," colonist Lewis W.

A nineteenth-century Mormon family

Shurtliff soon wrote, "near a small stream coming in from the east." The settlement of Limhi (originally named for a king mentioned in the Book of Mormon, but eventually called Lemhi) proved successful for a time. The Lemhi missionaries shared the tasks of planting and watering vegetable crops. More than one hundred Indians were baptized into the Mormon faith.

The Mormons' progress in settling the West began to make non-Mormons uneasy. The federal government disapproved of Brigham Young's attempts to override federal authorities. The trappers and mountaineers in the region began to fear an unbridled expansion of Mormonism. Finally, United States troops marched into Utah to take official control of that territory. Conflicts with the Indians forced the people of Lemhi to abandon their settlement in 1858.

Mormon interest in the wild Idaho country continued, however. On April 14, 1860, twenty-three Mormon families crossed Utah's northern border into present-day Idaho. On a bluff overlooking

Miners poured into Idaho after gold was discovered there in the 1860s.

the Cub River in the Cache Valley, the pioneers unpacked their wagons. Beneath the springtime sun, they cleared the land, planted crops, and built log cabins. Their little town of Franklin became Idaho's first permanent white settlement.

The hardworking people of Franklin dug irrigation ditches and showed that the dry soil of southern Idaho could be farmed. Other Mormon pioneers soon settled in the Bear Lake Valley and the Malad Valley regions. With these early settlements, Idaho at last became more than a brief stopping place for travelers.

GOLD!

In the 1850s, California's goldfields yielded dazzling riches to some lucky miners. Disappointed fortune hunters, however, turned their attention to other untouched lands. In 1860, Elias D.

Pierce snuck a party of ten prospectors into northern Idaho. The grizzled miners blazed a path across the reservation lands of the Nez Perce until they reached Orofino Creek in the Clearwater River region. "On the 1st of October commenced our labor," Pierce afterward declared. "Found gold in every place in the stream—I never saw a party of men so excited; they made the hills and mountains ring with shouts of joy."

News of gold brought miners rushing from California and Oregon. Already a work crew commanded by army Lieutenant John Mullen was hacking a military road across northern Idaho's Bitterroot Mountains. Steamboats churned their way up the Columbia and Snake rivers to the new Idaho-border boomtown of Lewiston. Using these routes, miners, merchants, tradesmen, and excitement-seekers poured into the Clearwater district.

Those who arrived too late to stake a claim near the mining town of Pierce searched elsewhere. Orofino, Elk City, Warren, Florence, and other Clearwater mining camps sprang up as quickly as prospectors could pitch their tents. Miners at one claim near Florence recovered $6,000 worth of ore in just two days. The merest whisper of a rumor of gold sent the miners stampeding. Rich discoveries farther south in the Boise Basin region brought nearly sixteen thousand gold seekers to such new mining towns as Idaho City, Rocky Bar, and Atlanta. By 1866, the Boise Basin strikes had yielded more than $24 million in gold.

THE MINER'S LIFE

Crouched beside Idaho's mountain streams, lonely prospectors carefully swirled gravel and water out of pans, searching for a glint of gold. Other miners gently rocked gravel and water through the strainers of short wooden "cradles." Some prospectors sent river water pouring through a series of long wooden boxes called *sluices*. Dirt shoveled into these sluices also washed through strainers, sometimes leaving flecks of gold behind.

Placer miners used a different method of finding gold. They sprayed high-pressure streams of water to wash away the soil in places where veins of ore lay near the surface of the ground. Muscled miners directing jets of water through huge nozzles watched entire hillsides break up quickly and disappear.

Gold veins often traveled deep into the heart of a mountain. When miners discovered such lodes of gold-bearing rock, they dug tunnels to reach it. Lode-mining operations required many workers and were usually run as companies. In the 1870s, a stream called Yankee Fork was the site of two of Idaho's earliest and most famous gold mines: the Charles Dickens and the General Custer. The miners blasted the rock with explosives, crushed it with heavy stone grinders called *arrastras*, and finally smelted the gold ore into pure, shining bars.

The men who caught "gold fever" and swarmed into Idaho during these years were a tough, independent breed. Few men brought their wives and children to take up the miner's difficult life. Mining towns always seemed filled with the wildest excitement. In Florence, one miner observed on a Sunday in 1862, "On almost every corner an auctioneer is selling horses, goods and merchandise of every sort. Great clumps of people stand in the streets discussing the 'new diggings.' The saloons are full of people. . . . Not infrequently some drunken ruffian draws his revolver and begins to shoot in the midst of the vast crowd. . . ." Thieves, gamblers, and murderers stole the miners' hard-earned money at every opportunity. Shooting battles sometimes erupted at disputed mining claims.

Boise as it appeared in 1866

Honest miners demanded law and justice in the region. United States troopers quelled violence in some camps. In other mining towns, prospectors elected sheriffs and courthouses were built. Finally, on March 4, 1863, President Abraham Lincoln officially established a territorial government in the region. The new Idaho Territory included the lands of present-day Idaho, Montana, and most of present-day Wyoming.

FATE OF THE INDIANS

"It is not expected that wild and warlike people will tamely submit to the occupation of their country by another race," warned Fort Hall Indian agent James Doty. Unfortunately, few whites made any attempt to understand the Indians or their culture. The surge of settlers into Idaho totally disrupted the Indians' way of life. As early as the 1850s, white-owned cattle headed along the Oregon Trail began depleting Shoshone and Bannock grazing lands. Before long, ranchers, whose livestock provided meat for the miners, claimed millions of other acres.

During the Nez Perce War, the Nez Perce were chased by United States troops through Idaho, Wyoming, and Montana as they tried to flee to safety in Canada.

In the early 1860s, angry and sometimes starving Indians attacked wagon trains and stole horses with increasing frequency. In early 1863, California militia commanded by Colonel Patrick Connor marched into southern Idaho to put an end to Shoshone raids along the wagon-train routes. On January 29, the ruthless soldiers pounced upon the winter encampment of the Cache Valley Shoshone near Bear River. Bullets whistled through the air during the fierce fighting. Afterward, settler William Hull walked the battlefield. "Never will I forget the scene, dead bodies were everywhere . . . all in all we counted nearly 400; two-thirds of this number being women and children."

Their spirit broken, most of the southern Idaho Shoshone and Bannock Indians moved onto the Fort Hall Reservation, an area set aside for them by the federal government. In 1878, a group of Bannock and Lemhi Shoshone journeyed north after obtaining permission to collect camas bulbs for food. At the Big Camas Prairie, these Indians discovered that the rooting hogs, cattle, and horses of white homesteaders had destroyed the natural camas crop. Facing starvation, the Native Americans attacked settlements and supply posts for food until pursuing soldiers killed, captured, or dispersed them, ending the brief Bannock War.

THE NEZ PERCE WAR

To gain more land, white settlers forced unfair treaties upon the Nez Perce people. In June of 1877, General O. O. Howard ordered a band of Nez Perce to move from their homeland in Oregon's beautiful Wallowa Valley to the Lapwai Reservation in Idaho. Nez Perce leader Chief Joseph, however, resisted resettlement. "If we ever owned the land, we still own it," he insisted. Even so, he and his people reluctantly started out for Lapwai. They never arrived, however. Along the way, a group of bitter Nez Perce warriors attacked some settlers, touching off a war between the Indians and the United States Army.

At White Bird Canyon and along the Clearwater River, the outnumbered Nez Perce successfully fought off blue-clad United States soldiers. Then, to escape from the army, they decided to flee to freedom and safety in Canada. In need of food and rest, the Indians hurried on their way. Over mountains and rivers, the American troops chased after them. After every bloody skirmish, the Nez Perce managed to escape. Slipping through the Targhee Pass, Chief Joseph led his people across Wyoming and northward into Montana.

For three and a half months, the Nez Perce journeyed through the wilderness. At the end of September, after trekking nearly 1,300 miles (2,092 kilometers), the weary band stopped to rest near the Bear Paw Mountains of present-day Montana. They were just 30 miles (48 kilometers) south of the Canadian border. Suddenly, 600 soldiers commanded by Colonel Nelson Miles surrounded the Indians. After a violent fight, Chief Joseph knew he was defeated. Riding into Miles's camp, the Nez Perce leader surrendered the 409 men, women and children who remained in his dwindling band. "Our chiefs are killed. . . . ," he exclaimed. "It is cold and we have no blankets. The little children are freezing to death. . . . Hear me, my chiefs! I am tired. My heart is sick and sad. From where the sun now stands, I will fight no more forever."

THE ROCKY ROAD TO STATEHOOD

Idaho's years as a United States territory were ones of constant change and political turmoil. In 1864, Congress voted to form the new Montana Territory and to extend the Dakota Territory, measures that greatly reduced the size of Idaho. The additional creation of the Wyoming Territory in 1868 lopped off another section of eastern Idaho, at last setting its borders as they are today.

By the 1860s, the lure of gold in southern Idaho had turned Boise into the territory's population center. In 1864, the growing city was chosen as the permanent capital. While stonemasons erected government buildings there, territorial legislators tried to hammer together laws. Settlers in northern Idaho deeply resented the loss of Lewiston as capital, and threatened repeatedly to annex their region to the state of Washington. The many Democrats living in Idaho disliked the territorial governors appointed by Republican United States presidents. Bitter political battles often strangled the territorial government's progress.

Even so, Idaho progressed. Advances in transportation brought civilization to remote regions of the territory. Stagecoaches and freight wagons carrying new homesteaders and merchandise

An authentic Idaho "mud wagon" stagecoach at the Idaho Transportation Museum in Boise

bounced along rutted roads. The sound of steamboat whistles brought excited settlers to the banks of the Snake River and the shores of Lake Pend Oreille and Coeur d'Alene Lake to hear the latest news. In 1874, both the Northern Pacific and the Union Pacific railroads began building branch lines into Idaho to gain access to mines and ranches. As a result, produce and passengers moved much more quickly, and new commercial cities such as Pocatello, American Falls, and Caldwell sprang up beside the tracks.

By 1890, nearly ninety thousand people had made Idaho their home. These Americans clamored for full national citizenship. Territorial delegate Fred T. Dubois presented Idaho's request for statehood to the United States Congress. "These people," proclaimed Dubois of his fellow Idahoans, "who have subdued the desert and the forest, who have wrenched untold millions from solemn and reluctant hills . . . who have borne the hardships which have opened up an empire . . . seek now by petition . . . the right of self-government." Congress responded speedily, and on July 3, 1890, Idaho was officially admitted to the Union. Territorial governor George L. Shoup was elected to be the first state governor, and proud Idahoans waved United States flags displaying the new forty-third star.

Chapter 6
ONE HUNDRED YEARS AND BEYOND

ONE HUNDRED YEARS AND BEYOND

RECLAIMING THE LAND

Water! Precious Water! What a glorious destiny,
The blood of the earth, of priceless worth, in this capacity
Was brought by dauntless pioneer, who worked with
ceaseless toil;
By hand and team, they made each stream, to quench this
thirsty soil.
—Idaho poet Rose Ward Scoresby

The first dutiful Mormons sent by Brigham Young into Idaho
faced incredible challenges. Most of the land they sought to
colonize was little more than a sun-parched sagebrush prairie that
stretched for hundreds of miles. In these desert lands, water
possessed a value even greater than gold. The Mormons used
every creek and stream to the fullest advantage. Sweating farmers
dug ditches and diverted the water in order to irrigate their lands.
Other settlers in the region followed their example.

In the 1880s, New York speculators dreamed of developing an
irrigation system to make dry land in the Boise River Valley
valuable. Engineer A. D. Foote designed a grand plan to construct
a 75-mile (121-kilometer) canal with more than 5,000 miles (8,047
kilometers) of ditches branching from its course. This project
progressed very slowly, however, because of its enormous cost.
Years passed as various work crews swung picks and shovels in
an effort to make the New York Canal a reality. Other private
attempts to bring water to the region also faced huge financial
difficulties.

Eventually, the United States government jumped in to help stalled irrigation projects and promote new ones. The 1894 Carey Act granted huge tracts of federal land to states that successfully completed irrigation programs. During the next thirty-five years, eager Idaho developers proposed dozens of ambitious projects. The Twin Falls South Side proposal, promoted by I. B. Perrine, proved by far Idaho's greatest success under the Carey Act. Using tractors, steam derricks, and other machinery, the project sent irrigated water streaming across more than 200,000 acres (80,938 hectares) by 1909.

The National Reclamation Act of 1902 provided for direct federal assistance to districts unable to build irrigation canals independently. Reorganized under this law, the New York Canal—renamed the Boise Project—opened officially in 1909, irrigating 300,000 acres (121,407 hectares). As other projects were also completed, new settlers hurried into southern Idaho to buy irrigated farm lots.

Even lands that were still arid attracted settlers to southern Idaho. In 1900, the federal government purchased 418,000 acres (169,160 hectares) from the Shoshone and Bannock Indians of the Fort Hall Reservation. It was opened for public settlement on June 17, 1902, sparking a huge land rush. Thousands of excited homesteaders scrambled out of Pocatello to stake claims.

MINING CLAIMS AND LABOR WARS

Many of Idaho's early gold towns faded when their mines stopped producing ore. Thousands of prospectors drifted away to search for riches elsewhere. Improved methods of smelting silver and lead increased the value of those minerals. Discoveries of silver and lead deposits in the Wood River area brought droves of fortune hunters scampering back to Idaho in 1880. Such mines as the Queen of the Hills, the Minnie Moore, and the Triumph yielded millions of dollars' worth of ore, and boomtowns such as Bellevue, Hailey, and Ketchum blossomed almost overnight.

In 1884, miners reported even more fabulous finds of silver, lead, and zinc farther north in the Coeur d'Alene Mountains. Such towns as Burke, Mullan, Wardner, and Kellogg sprang into existence as people rushed into Shoshone County. In time, the incredible wealth of the Coeur d'Alene region would account for 80 percent of Idaho's metal production. The richest mines, such as the Emma, the Last Chance, and the Bunker Hill and Sullivan, made their founders millionaires. With so much money at stake, developers and investors dragged each other into court to fight over mining claims. Old prospector Noah Kellogg, for example, spent years proving his rightful ownership of the Bunker Hill and Sullivan mine.

By 1890, nearly all of Idaho's mines had been sold to large, eastern corporations. These companies employed hundreds of miners and used the most modern machinery to recover ore from the ground. A collapse in national silver prices in 1892 sparked violence in the Coeur d'Alene region. On June 11, 1892, overworked miners, furious about pay cuts, marched to the town of Gem and dynamited the mill of the Frisco mine. Horrified by the destruction, Governor N. B. Willey declared martial law. Soldiers arrested hundreds of union miners in Shoshone County.

Labor strife broke out again in 1899. By that time, all of the Coeur d'Alene mine owners except the Bunker Hill and Sullivan owners recognized the union known as the Western Federation of Miners (WFM). Union organizers secretly called for a strike of the Bunker Hill and Sullivan in an attempt to force the mine to pay union-scale wages. On April 29, 1899, about a thousand angry

During the labor strife that rocked the Coeur d'Alene mining district in 1899, rebellious union miners were arrested and held in outdoor prisons that became known as "bullpens."

miners swept onto Bunker Hill and Sullivan property. They placed an explosive charge and watched gleefully as it blew the mine's concentrator to smithereens.

Outraged, Governor Frank Steunenberg called in United States troops once more. For months, hundreds of arrested union miners paced inside the barbed wire of large outdoor prisons that became known as "bullpens." By the time the Coeur d'Alene mines reopened, Steunenberg had broken the WFM in Idaho and won the hatred of miners throughout the state. Five years later, on December 30, 1905, the former governor opened a back gate at his home in Caldwell. It triggered a hidden bomb that mortally wounded him. "They finally got me, John," Steunenberg gasped to his brother, "it's the Coeur d'Alene. I can't live."

Police soon arrested miner Harry Orchard for Steunenberg's murder. Orchard confessed that vengeful officers of the Western Federation of Miners hired him to carry out the deed. In Colorado, detectives kidnapped William "Big Bill" Haywood and two other

WFM union leaders and brought them to Idaho to stand trial. The trial of Big Bill Haywood in Ada County attracted national attention. Famed lawyer Clarence Darrow defended the well-known union leader, while young Idaho attorney William Borah prosecuted the case. In the end, because of lack of evidence, the jury found Haywood not guilty of conspiracy.

WHIPSAWS AND WANIGANS

Axmen felled the trees, while loggers with whipsaws cut the boards that built Idaho's 1860s mining towns. In the years that followed, small, family-operated sawmills prospered as they filled Idaho's lumber needs. Then, in 1900, a number of successful Wisconsin and Minnesota lumbermen looked westward to Idaho for future opportunities. Investors such as Frederick Weyerhaeuser bought huge tracts of untouched pine forests in the mountains both north and south of the Clearwater River. Soon, seven major companies had laid claim to much of the state's timberlands. By 1906, President Theodore Roosevelt, an ardent conservationist, had halted further land purchases by placing most of Idaho's remaining forests under the protection of the U.S. Forest Service.

In the beginning, rough terrain and high transportation costs caused the state's logging industry to limp along without profit. The great fire of 1910 also stunned Idaho's lumbermen. That summer, hot, dry weather kindled hundreds of small fires. In August, a strong wind fanned the state into a raging furnace. Sheets of flame swept through the Bitterroot Mountains and other parts of Idaho and Montana. The blaze claimed eighty-five lives and scorched about 3 million acres (1.2 million hectares) of land before rain finally snuffed it out.

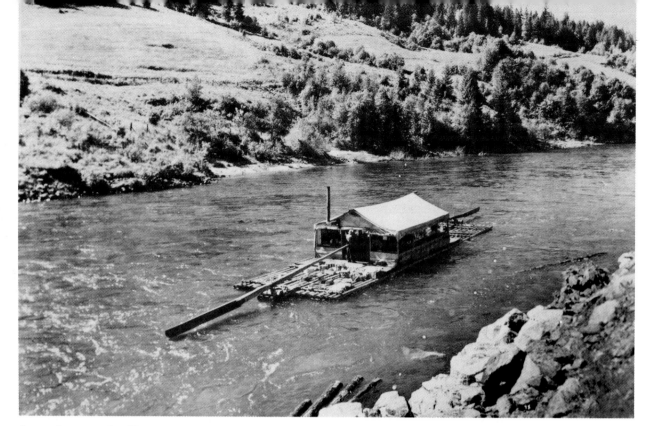

A wanigan on the Clearwater River

In spite of severe difficulties and repeated bad luck, Idaho's commercial lumbering industry gradually grew to surpass mining in importance. By 1920, the state's thick stands of pine were providing wood for housing and manufacturing across America. Crude logging roads and a few mountain railways brought much of the timber to market. However, loggers found that river runs often provided the easiest method of transportation to sawmills. Greased sluice chutes sent newly cut logs skidding down the mountainsides. From riverside loading areas, the logs were floated downstream. Balanced on the logs, expert loggers often broke up jams along the route. Others, rowing sturdy boats called *bateaus*, recovered lost or stranded logs. Behind all floated the company *wanigan*, a wooden raft equipped with a simple cookhouse to provide food for the logging crews.

PROGRESS AND PROSPERITY

The early 1900s began an era of progress and prosperity in Idaho. Under irrigation, the state's thirsty topsoil proved very fertile. Cattlemen and sheepherders sometimes clashed as they competed for valuable rangelands. Farmers planted such high-value crops as wheat, alfalfa, and sugar beets to supply eastern demand. The state's high elevation, as well as a climate that was hot in the day and cool at night, made potato growing ideal. Soon, acres of Idaho farmland yielded wagonloads of the finest potatoes anywhere to be found. The new orchards of the Payette Valley gained a reputation for producing fine fruit. In such towns as Fruitland, Indian Valley, and Mesa, the colorful blossoms of apple, cherry, and plum trees filled the air with their fragrant smells each spring.

To reclaim even more land, Idahoans organized a number of gigantic dam projects. Work began on the Snake River's great Minidoka Dam in 1904. The Milner Dam, as well as a dam at American Falls, also allowed more farming in the Snake River Valley. In 1915, engineers completed the Arrowrock Dam on the Boise River. At 351 feet (107 meters), it was the tallest dam in the world at the time. In addition to pumping water, the power stations at these and other dams generated more than enough electricity to meet Idaho's increasing demands.

Idaho's march toward progress extended to its government as well. In an effort to give a greater voice to Idaho's citizens, state politicians revised many laws between 1900 and 1920. New commissions, such as the state public utilities commission and the state highway commission, were designed to meet the needs of the people. Moses Alexander became the first Jewish governor in United States history when he was elected governor of Idaho in

In the 1900s, new methods of irrigation brought to life the fertile but
dry lands of southern Idaho.

1914. While in office, Alexander won an eight-hour workday and
higher wages for Idaho's loggers.

Idahoans sent Republican William Borah to Washington, D.C.
in 1907. During his thirty-three-year tenure as a United States
senator, Borah led the fight for such progressive measures as the
direct election of United States senators and the graduated income
tax. He sponsored the establishment of the United States
Department of Labor in 1913, and served with distinction for
eight years as chairman of the Senate Foreign Relations
Committee.

DEPRESSION AND WAR

Idaho's decades of prosperity ground to a sudden halt in 1919.
That year, a severe drought ruined crops. The dry weather also

sparked fires that destroyed thousands of acres of timber. In Europe, people cheered the end of World War I. Unfortunately, to meet war demands, many Idaho farmers had overextended production. Soon, produce glutted the market and farm prices collapsed. A bushel of Idaho potatoes that had sold for $1.51 in 1919, for example, was worth only $.31 in 1922.

Over the next few years, Idaho's farmers struggled to recover lost income. Hard times became even harder, however, when the entire nation spiraled into a severe economic depression after the great Wall Street stock market crash of 1929. Farm prices sank to all-time lows. Many farms and businesses failed; the mining and lumbering industries fared no better. Thousands of people, suddenly unemployed, roamed city streets and hiked country roads searching for work.

The 1932 election of United States President Franklin D. Roosevelt brought some help to Idahoans. Many of President Roosevelt's "New Deal" programs were implemented in the state. More federal money was spent bringing electricity to rural Idaho than to any other state. Federally funded public-works projects put Idahoans to work constructing more than two hundred schools, libraries, and other public buildings. The New Deal's Civilian Conservation Corps (CCC) proved especially popular in Idaho. By 1939, some eighteen thousand young men had journeyed to Idaho to live and work at seventy CCC fresh-air camps. These recruits improved country roads, built campgrounds, and assisted in forestry projects. To save Idaho's farmers from ruin, the federal government granted loans and assistance totaling over $120 million during these trying years.

The country's need to gear up for World War II brought the Great Depression to an end. On December 7, 1941, soaring Japanese warplanes bombed the United States naval base at Pearl

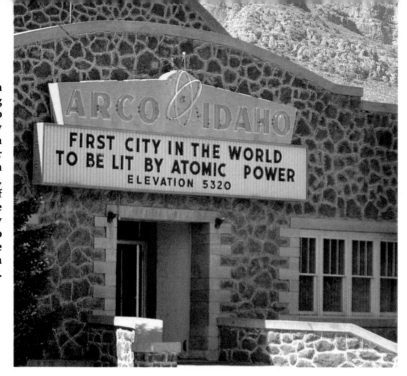

In 1951, at a reactor testing station near Idaho Falls, electricity was generated from nuclear energy for the first time in history. In 1955, the nearby town of Arco became the first community in the world to receive its entire power supply from nuclear energy.

FIRST CITY IN THE WORLD
TO BE LIT BY ATOMIC POWER
ELEVATION 5320

Harbor, Hawaii. Congress responded to this surprise attack by declaring war on Japan and its German and Italian allies. Fear of spies and further sneak attacks led to a regrettable chapter in American history. Thousands of Japanese Americans living along the Pacific coast were ordered by the federal government to move to relocation camps further inland in Oregon, California, and Idaho. One such camp was the Minidoka Relocation Center, built at Hunt in Jerome County. In August 1942, the first of some ten thousand Japanese American evacuees entered its gates. These people lived out most of the war behind barbed-wire fences in tar-papered barracks, prisoners within their own country.

The government shipped captured German and Italian prisoners of war to Idaho, as well. At remote camps near Rupert and Nampa, these enemy soldiers were often sent out to work on local farms. Several United States military bases in Idaho provided training for the armed services during the war. The air force established major airfields at Boise, Mountain Home, and Pocatello. The War Department built the nation's second-largest naval-training station at Lake Pend Oreille. Before the war's end, an astonishing 293,000 navy recruits had graduated from the Farragut Naval Base.

Idaho's miners contributed to the war effort by producing record amounts of lead, zinc, tungsten, and other essential metals for industrial use. Idaho's farmers worked diligently to meet the nation's increased demands for food supplies. Many other Idahoans worked in factories that produced munitions and other military supplies. By 1945, through the patriotic effort of its people, the state had made an economic recovery.

THE RISE OF MODERN IDAHO

The dropping by the United States of atomic bombs on the enemy cities of Hiroshima and Nagasaki stunned the Japanese into complete surrender in August 1945. Idahoans cheered the arrival of peace, and Idaho soon played an active role in the beginning of the nuclear age. In 1949, America's new Atomic Energy Commission established what is now called the Idaho National Engineering Laboratory (INEL) on 900 square miles (2,331 square kilometers) of desert land between Idaho Falls and Arco. On December 20, 1951, INEL made world history when its power plant became the first to produce electricity by using atomic energy. Over the years, INEL's physicists continued to conduct important reactor research, including the development of nuclear submarines for the United States Navy.

Idaho's government did much to assist the state's growth in the postwar period. In the late 1940s, the state legislature streamlined many state agencies and improved its state educational system. In 1954, Republican Robert E. Smylie began what was to be a twelve-year tenure as governor. Smylie's administration oversaw the

A memorial has been built to honor the ninety-one miners who perished in the 1972 Sunshine mine disaster.

further modernizing of such agencies as the state health system and the state parks system.

Idaho continued to make advances in both agriculture and industry. J. R. Simplot, for example, began filling military contracts for dried onions and potatoes in 1942. After the war, Simplot looked for ways to widen his markets. Researchers at his Caldwell headquarters soon developed frozen french fries, instant mashed potatoes, and other processed foods. Geologists discovered that Idaho was rich with deposits of phosphate, a valuable fertilizer. Through the 1950s and 1960s, Simplot and others successfully developed phosphate mines in the Fort Hall region. Improved fertilization methods, sprinkling systems, and other new farming techniques produced better and bigger Idaho crops and made the Idaho potato truly famous.

Hardworking Idahoans expanded their state's lumbering

Eleven people were killed and millions of dollars' worth of property was destroyed when the Teton Dam burst in 1976.

industry. At the same time, the state's untouched forests and many natural wonders attracted growing numbers of vacationers. As a result, recreational-vehicle factories and mobile-home plants proved successful new industries in Idaho. The rapid growth of tourism in Idaho led to an increasing desire to preserve the state's natural attractions. Since the 1960s, Idahoans have tried hard to balance agricultural and industrial progress with careful conservation.

Some environmentalists still complain that the huge Dworshak Dam, completed on the Clearwater River in 1973, was unnecessary and damaged the region's ecology. The poorly located Teton River Dam brought even greater grief to Idahoans. On June 5, 1976, the dam burst suddenly, and 80 billion gallons (303 billion liters) of water surged south across the countryside. "The sound was just like a roar," exclaimed one witness, "like we were standing at the bottom of a waterfall." The ensuing flood destroyed hundreds of homes in Sugar City, Rexburg, Idaho Falls, and other towns along its path. On farmlands, cattle drowned and topsoil washed away. Following the Teton Dam disaster, the state vowed to examine future dam projects far more carefully.

Idaho's miners had suffered a terrible tragedy a few years earlier. On May 2, 1972, fire broke out below the 3,100-foot (945-meter) level of the Sunshine mine near Wardner. Deadly smoke quickly filled the maze of tunnels. As trapped miners choked and searched for escape routes, rescue crews made heroic efforts to save them. Although eighty-two miners survived, the disaster claimed the lives of ninety-one men.

CHALLENGES FOR TOMORROW

"If the people here trust you, they'll vote for you, even if they don't agree with you down the line," declared Idaho senator Frank Church. Following in the progressive tradition of William Borah, Church was first elected to the United States Senate in 1956. For the next twenty-four years, the Democrat served Idaho's voters in an honest manner that earned their trust. Regarded as a Senate "dove" because of his outspoken criticism of American involvement in the war in Vietnam in the 1960s, Church also made an impact as a member of the Senate Foreign Relations Committee.

While in Washington, D.C., Church sponsored a number of important conservation bills that affected Idahoans. The National Wild and Scenic Rivers Act of 1968 and the creation of the Sawtooth National Recreation Area, for example, preserved sections of Idaho's majestic wilderness for coming generations.

Elected governor of Idaho in 1970, Democrat Cecil Andrus also pushed strongly for conservation. Andrus recognized that new fish hatcheries and the development of wildlife programs would attract more tourism and thus benefit the state. In 1977, President Jimmy Carter chose Andrus to be the United States secretary of the interior. For the next four years, Andrus oversaw the protection of the entire country's national parks and lands.

Perhaps the greatest problem facing present-day Idahoans is the danger of toxic waste. Many Idahoans support the use of nuclear

In the 1960s, Idaho Senator Frank Church pushed through legislation that ensured the preservation of many of Idaho's scenic wilderness areas.

energy. Others, however, feel that the hazards of nuclear plants can no longer be ignored. In 1988, the United States Department of Energy revealed that the Idaho National Engineering Laboratory was one of the most contaminated nuclear-weapons-industry sites in the nation. The report triggered fears that radioactive waste was seeping into the Snake River water system. The INEL's plan to build four new nuclear reactors brought vocal protesters and supporters to public hearings.

Parades, fireworks, fairs, and festivals filled the state's 1990 calendar as Idaho prepared to celebrate its first one hundred years of statehood. Idahoans could look back proudly at all they had achieved and all they had preserved. Though Lewis and Clark might not recognize some of Idaho today, the state's most distinctive features remain the same—and hopefully always will.

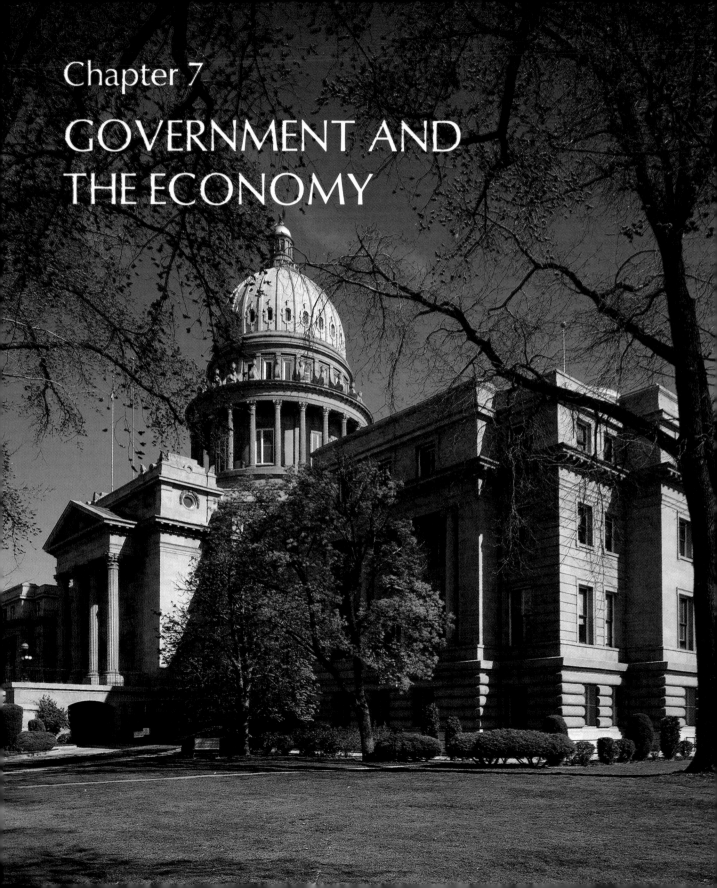

Chapter 7

GOVERNMENT AND THE ECONOMY

GOVERNMENT AND THE ECONOMY

The success of a state is measured by the accomplishments of its government and the health of its economy. Idaho's government and businesses work side by side as they strive for continued growth and progress.

STATE GOVERNMENT

In the summer of 1889, Idaho politicians gathered in Boise and wrote a constitution for the new state they hoped to form. Although amended many times since then, that document still governs Idaho today. Like the federal government, Idaho's government is divided into three branches. The legislative branch creates and repeals the laws. The judicial branch, or court system, interprets the laws. The executive branch, or office of the governor, sees that the laws are carried out.

Idaho's legislature consists of two separate chambers. The senate has forty-two members; the house of representatives has eighty-four members. The legislature votes bills into law and assists the governor in designing the budget and legislative programs. By electing their legislators to two-year terms, the voters of Idaho's thirty-three legislative districts assure themselves a voice in state affairs.

Idaho's voters elect the five members of the Idaho Supreme Court to six-year terms. They also elect eleven lower district-court judges to four-year terms. Dressed in solemn black robes, these judges listen to court cases and rule on the proper meanings of the state's laws.

The governor of Idaho serves a four-year term and may be reelected an unlimited number of times. The governor controls state spending, oversees the operation of state agencies, and is the state's chief law-enforcement officer. A surprising 63.7 percent of Idaho's land is federally owned, more than in any other state except Alaska. Therefore, the governor often works closely with the United States government. Federal grants account for almost one-third of Idaho's yearly budget. Sales taxes, personal and corporate income taxes, and a gasoline tax also provide revenue for the state.

EDUCATION

"Adopt-a-Caribou," offered John Gahl, education coordinator of Idaho's Fish and Game Department. In 1986, the state decided to reintroduce that endangered species into the Selkirk Mountains, where vast herds once roamed. Schoolchildren throughout northern Idaho jumped at Gahl's invitation to get involved. In selected classrooms, students decorated the transmitter collar that would be worn by their special caribou. Each class gave its caribou a name, such as "Radar" or "Selkirk Sal." Captured in Canada, the first group of twenty-four caribou were released in Idaho in the spring of 1987. Since then, each class has closely followed the progress of its adopted animal. "We are letting the caribou do the teaching," Gahl explained proudly, "how they migrate, wildlife biology, . . . map-reading skills, [and] wildlife conservation of endangered species. It's a good learning experience."

Young people in Idaho have been hungry to learn ever since Henry and Eliza Spalding opened the region's first Indian mission

Boise State University

The University of Idaho at Moscow

school in 1836. During pioneer days, settlers often bought subscriptions so their children could attend simple log-cabin schools. Today, some 115 local school districts provide fine public education for more than 210,000 students from kindergarten through twelfth grade.

Well over half of Idaho's high-school graduates continue their education at colleges and technical schools. "We have about as much use for a university in Idaho as there is for a fifth wheel of a wagon," the *Idaho Daily Statesman* predicted in 1889. The University of Idaho, which opened soon after in Moscow, proved that newspaper very wrong. Through the years, agricultural programs at the university, for example, have developed hardy new crop varieties of wheat, barley, oats, and peas, all of which have benefited farmers tremendously.

Idaho's many other institutions of higher learning contribute greatly to the state, as well. Among the state's publicly funded

Lewiston, which lies at the confluence of the Snake and Clearwater rivers, is the farthest-inland seaport in the western United States.

colleges are Idaho State University, at Pocatello; Boise State University, at Boise; Lewis-Clark State College, at Lewiston; North Idaho Junior College, at Coeur d'Alene; and the College of Southern Idaho, at Twin Falls. Outstanding private learning centers in the state include the College of Idaho, at Caldwell; Northwest Nazarene College, at Nampa; and Ricks College, a junior college in Rexburg.

TRANSPORTATION AND COMMUNICATION

"Steep and Stoney our men and horses much fatigued," wrote William Clark in September 1805. Today, travelers on U.S. Highway 12 follow the path of Lewis and Clark through the Bitterroot Mountains and along the Lochsa River with much more ease and comfort. An even larger highway, Interstate 90, also carries east-west traffic across the Idaho Panhandle. In the south, drivers crossing the state most often rely on Interstate 84, which approximates the route of the old Oregon Trail. U.S. Highway 95 is the state's main north-south highway.

In all, some 63,000 miles (101,386 kilometers) of roads thread through Idaho's mountains, valleys, and plains. Two transcontinental railroads also provide commercial service through Idaho. Amtrak provides passenger service in the state. Idaho wheat growers and lumbermen still use river transportation, as well. In 1975, engineers completed the Columbia-Snake River Inland Waterway. Stretching 700 miles (1,127 kilometers) to the Pacific Ocean, the waterway makes Lewiston the farthest-inland seaport in the West. Boise and Idaho's other large cities offer regular airline service.

Communication has always played a valuable role in Idaho. Today, seventy-two newspapers are published in the state, thirteen of them dailies. Boise citizens have been buying copies of the *Idaho Statesman* since 1864. Other leading papers include the *Tribune* of Lewiston, the Coeur d'Alene *Press*, the Idaho Falls *Post-Register*, the Twin Falls *Times-News*, and Pocatello's *Idaho State Journal*.

Idaho's first radio station, KFAU, started broadcasting in Boise in 1922. Viewers began watching the state's first television station, Boise's KIDO (now KTVB), in 1953. Currently, more than ninety Idaho radio stations and twelve television stations provide the state with entertaining and educational programming.

AGRICULTURE

Some twenty-four thousand farms sprawl across the landscape of Idaho. Though bank debts, droughts, and even plagues of

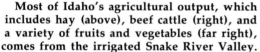
Most of Idaho's agricultural output, which includes hay (above), beef cattle (right), and a variety of fruits and vegetables (far right), comes from the irrigated Snake River Valley.

grasshoppers have ruined some farmers in recent years, the state's agricultural production remains impressive.

Potatoes, of course, are Idaho's best-known crop. In fact, Idaho grows more potatoes than any other state. Idaho potatoes, most of which are of the hardy and tasty Russet Burbank variety, account for 25 percent of the nation's total production. Most Idaho potatoes are grown in the Snake River region. Idaho also ranks among the top five states in annual production of barley, sugar beets, hops, mint, dry beans, and onions. Other valued crops include dried peas, lentils, sweet corn, wheat, and alfalfa. At harvest times, orchard owners to the west of Boise pick huge quantities of fruit. Only three states produce more plums and

prunes than Idaho. Cherries, apples, and peaches are also grown in the state.

Livestock represents a large portion of Idaho's agricultural output. Growing numbers of sheep, lambs, and cattle graze on the state's ranch lands or are fattened in feedlot pens. Idaho's dairy farms are concentrated in the Snake River Valley. Hog, poultry, and egg production also add to farm income. State and national streams are stocked with the nearly 5 million trout raised each year by hatchery workers in Hagerman. The 25 million pounds (11 million kilograms) of trout raised yearly at the huge commercial hatchery north of Buhl also helps make Idaho the nation's leader in trout production.

Idaho's dense, abundant forests have made the state a major center for lumbering and the manufacture of wood products.

MANUFACTURING AND SERVICE INDUSTRIES

Idaho's Indians once used the trees around them to build dwellings and fashion canoes. They wove the tree bark into clothing and colorful mats and baskets, and brewed medicines out of buds and twigs. Today, the harvesting of Idaho's forests provides lumber companies with valuable wood for construction, pulp, paper products, and packaging materials. The largest timber company headquartered in Idaho is the Boise Cascade Corporation. Boise Cascade, the Potlatch Corporation, and other successful Idaho lumber companies employ thousands of workers at logging camps, sawmills, particleboard plants, and pulping plants across the state.

Food processing has been a leading industry in Idaho ever since the J. R. Simplot Company led the way in the 1940s. Today, food processing is Idaho's leading industry. Each year, Simplot sells

Idaho's many potato-processing plants transform the state's leading crop into food products that are enjoyed throughout the nation.

millions of pounds of french fries to the McDonald's restaurant chain. Frozen potatoes processed by the Ore-Ida Company are sold nationwide, as well. Fruit and vegetable canning factories operate throughout Idaho. Nampa boasts the nation's largest beet-sugar refinery.

The chemical and computer-component industries have grown in the state in recent years. Other Idaho companies provide important services. The Morrison-Knudsen Construction Company, based in Boise, is one of the nation's largest construction companies. Difficult dam and road-building projects keep its engineers busy worldwide. A huge supermarket chain also got its start in Idaho. Joseph Albertson opened his first supermarket in Boise in 1939. By 1986, his company operated 452 stores in 17 western and southern states.

Idaho is the nation's leading producer of silver.

NATURAL RESOURCES

It is not surprising that Idaho's nickname is the Gem State. More than eighty varieties of gemstones are found within its borders. The state chose the star garnet as its official gemstone. When polished, the dark blue stone shines with a starry lustre. Each year, placer mines at Clarkia produce some 13,000 tons (11,793 metric tons) of garnet-sand for industrial use as an abrasive.

The prospectors who swarmed into Idaho in the 1860s discovered mineral riches that still abound today. Rapidly changing metal prices and high operating costs have closed some mines, however. The state's mining population now numbers less than four thousand. Even so, the roar of huge electric shovels and

An Idaho plant where phosphate rock is processed into fertilizer

the crunching noise of massive concentrators testify that the work goes on. At the Lucky Friday mine near Mullan, engineers sank a new 7,700-foot- (2,347-meter-) deep silver shaft in the early 1980s. Today it helps make the Coeur d'Alene district the largest silver producer in the world.

Idaho is the nation's fifth-leading producer of lead and zinc. The state's wealth of natural resources also includes such newer metals as cadmium, tungsten, vanadium, and molybdenum, all used in the manufacture of steel. Idaho stones such as basalt, pumice, and perlite are used extensively by the construction industries. Each year, the Shoshone-Bannock allow the mining of tons of phosphate rock on the Fort Hall Indian Reservation. Crushed and treated, Idaho phosphate fertilizers enrich the soil of farms throughout the nation and the world.

Chapter 8
CULTURE AND RECREATION

CULTURE AND RECREATION

*Now Paul Bunyan had to fall back on a last plan. . . . This was to
build a great sled . . . and have Babe, the blue ox, haul the loggers
to and from work each day. It was a desperate plan, and no one but
Paul Bunyan would have had the courage to attempt it. It must be
remembered that the blue ox measured forty-two ax handles and a
plug of chewing tobacco between the horns; an ordinary man at his
front had to use a telescope to see what he was doing with his hind
legs, he was so long.*
—from *Paul Bunyan* by James Stevens

LITERATURE

As a young man, James Stevens drove mule teams in the
logging camps around Weiser, Idaho. In the evenings, he listened
as the loggers entertained each other with fantastic stories about a
giant lumberjack named Paul Bunyan. Years later, Stevens sat
down and wrote a collection of these tall tales. His extremely
successful book *Paul Bunyan*, published in 1925, made Paul
Bunyan and his blue ox, Babe, beloved figures in American
folklore.

Nearly a century earlier, well-known New York writer
Washington Irving (author of "Rip Van Winkle" and "The
Legend of Sleepy Hollow") helped make the Idaho region famous.
In 1836, after gathering information from Wilson Hunt Price and
other western explorers, he penned *Astoria*, about John Jacob
Astor's Northwest fur trade. The same year, Irving published *The
Adventures of Captain Bonneville*, a very popular account of
Benjamin Bonneville's travels. The romance and excitement of

Portraits of Ezra Pound (left)
and James Stevens (above)

these two books encouraged many Americans to journey west and
see the Idaho territory for themselves.

In 1884, Mary Hallock Foote accompanied her husband, a civil
engineer, to the Boise Valley. While living in the state over the
next twelve years, Mrs. Foote wrote such popular western novels
as *John Bodewin's Testimony* and *The Chosen Valley*. Her many short
stories also described life in Idaho. Illustrated with her fine pen-
and-ink sketches, the stories appeared in such national magazines
as *Century*, *Scribner's*, and *St. Nicholas*.

In the town of Hailey stands the house where poet Ezra Pound
was born in 1885. Pound, who lived in Europe during most of his
adult life, was a controversial figure because of his Fascist politics
and eccentric ideals. The literary genius of such works as *Cantos*,
however, influenced many of the twentieth century's greatest
writers, and will continue to influence many generations to come.

In 1935, the federal government's Works Progress
Administration (WPA) decided to publish thorough guidebooks
of the states. Boise novelist Vardis Fisher was chosen to write the

book about Idaho. Fisher's complete *Idaho Guide*, published in 1937, was the first in the series to be completed. Afterwards, other WPA state-guide writers were instructed to use Fisher's fine work as their model. Fisher was also the author of *Mountain Man*, on which the movie *Jeremiah Johnson* was based.

The grave of Nobel-Prizewinning writer Ernest Hemingway lies in Ketchum, Idaho. "A helluva lot of state, this Idaho, that I didn't know about," declared Hemingway during his first visit in 1939. By that time, the forty-year-old writer's reputation as a creator of tersely styled novels and stories was already established. During fall hunting vacations between 1939 and 1941, Hemingway lived at Ketchum's Sun Valley Lodge and finished his novel of the Spanish Civil War, *For Whom the Bell Tolls*. A great outdoorsman, Hemingway chose to make Ketchum his permanent home in 1959. Plagued by physical illness and a troubled mind, however, Hemingway shot himself on July 2, 1961. Today, engraved upon a Hemingway memorial in Ketchum are words the famous author once wrote to eulogize an Idaho friend: "Best of all he loved the fall . . . the leaves yellow on the cottonwoods, leaves floating on the trout streams and above the hills the high blue windless skies. . . . Now he will be part of them forever."

ART AND MUSIC

Idaho's ancient Indians left simple rock paintings and carvings that still survive. More-recent artists have also found inspiration in Idaho. Folk-art exhibits bring visitors to the Boise Gallery of Art. In the 1880s, Margaretta Brown and George W. Russell both painted colorful scenes depicting Idaho's progress. Thomas Moran painted canvases that captured the beauty of Idaho's wild landscape for all time.

A musical concert during the annual Festival at Sandpoint

A remarkable equestrian statue of George Washington stands at an honored spot inside the state capitol building. It was completed in 1869 by Charles Ostner. Using crude tools and guided only by a postage stamp featuring Washington, he spent four years carving the statue from a huge log of ponderosa pine.

Sculptor Gutzon Borglum was born in a cabin near St. Charles in 1867. In the 1930s, Borglum achieved national fame when he carved giant renderings of the faces of Washington, Jefferson, Lincoln, and Theodore Roosevelt at Mount Rushmore in South Dakota.

Music soothed even the roughest pioneers of early Idaho. In mining towns such as Silver City and Idaho City, prospectors packed the seats of concert halls to listen to classical music and operas. Today the Boise Philharmonic, the Idaho Falls Symphony, and several university orchestras still attract crowds whenever they perform.

The National Oldtime Fiddlers Contest is held annually in Weiser.

Perhaps more important is Idaho's rich folk-music tradition. Such folk songs as "The Girl Named Ida-Ho," "Eagle Rock," "Grand Idaho," and "A Prospector's Song" are uniquely Idahoan. Many versions of the charming ballad "Way Out in Idaho" exist, including one with the following chorus:

> Way out in Idaho,
> We're coming to Idaho,
> With a four-horse team we'll soon be seen,
> Way out in Idaho.

The love of folk music in the state is evidenced at fairs and festivals throughout the year. Boise holds a Music Week every May, and plenty of folk music is included in the program. Each June, people head for Weiser to witness the exciting competition at the National Oldtime Fiddlers Contest. Those who appreciate traditional Basque music and dancing regularly attend the Sheepherder's Ball, held each year in Boise. Idaho's Swedish American population keeps its special heritage alive with singing and accordion music at the New Sweden Pioneer Day picnic held in July near Idaho Falls. The Lionel Hampton Jazz Festival, which is held each year in Moscow and is the largest jazz assembly concert in the Northwest, features some of the world's top jazz musicians.

SPORTS AND RECREATION

Although the state has no major-league teams of its own, over the years it has provided the nation with several sports stars. Harmon Killebrew of Payette slugged 573 home runs during his professional baseball career. That statistic earned him a place in the Baseball Hall of Fame in 1984. Meridian native Vernon Law spent sixteen years pitching for the Pittsburgh Pirates. Idaho's Larry Jackson also enjoyed a long baseball career in the National League. Another Idahoan, famous all-pro guard Jerry Kramer, jolted his opponents during a successful football career with the Green Bay Packers.

"I remember vividly getting out of the [railroad] car in Ketchum. I put on my skis and skied into Sun Valley on this powder snow. . . . I fell in love with the place then and there." Union Pacific Railroad tycoon W. Averell Harriman never forgot his first visit to the area where he developed and opened a fabulous ski lodge in 1936. Ever since, the resort has attracted vacationers who love downhill and cross-country skiing, ice skating, and other winter sports. Sun Valley is one of eighteen ski resorts that thrive in Idaho today. The state also boasts 5,000 miles (8,047 kilometers) of groomed trails for snowmobilers.

In recent years, tourism has become a major industry in Idaho. The state offers almost every kind of outdoor activity imaginable. "Idaho bird shooting is the best in the world," marveled Ernest

Skiers in Sun Valley

Hemingway in 1939. Pheasant, grouse, quail, ducks, and geese are among the many varieties of fowl stalked by hunters. Licensed sportsmen also hunt bigger game in season, such as deer, elk, moose, antelope, mountain goats, and bighorn sheep. Idaho's streams and lakes are an angler's delight. Fishing enthusiasts reel in bass, perch, bluegill, catfish, and several kinds of salmon. World-record-size trout have been hooked on Lake Pend Oreille. Conservationists have been instrumental in helping to preserve Idaho's wildlife and natural wonders for tourists and natives alike.

Through spring, summer, and fall, backpackers hike along Idaho's craggy mountain trails and camp beneath towering pines. Many Boise citizens enjoy escaping to Stanley, Redfish, and Alturas lakes in the Sawtooth National Recreation Area, where they can enjoy sailing, canoeing, and swimming. The sports of kayaking and river-rafting bring thrill seekers to the white-water

Silver Creek is world famous for its huge trout.

rapids of the Selway, Salmon, Snake, and other Idaho rivers. Nineteen state parks offer tourists fine outdoor settings for relaxation. A narrow strip of Yellowstone National Park stretches along Idaho's southeastern border.

Natural hot springs bubble up in many places in southern Idaho. Indians and settlers have enjoyed their soothing warmth for centuries. At the resort at Lava Hot Springs, for example, visitors romp in natural mineral waters that remain a constant 110 degrees Fahrenheit (43 degrees Celsius). The Gem State offers rock hounds plenty of interesting rock formations to investigate. Enthusiastic spelunkers can creep through caves that are millions of years old. Horseback riding is one of the most pleasant activities enjoyed in Idaho. Hardy cowboys and cowgirls show off their roping and broncobusting skills at many rodeos held throughout the state. For people desiring fresh air and open country, Idaho is paradise on earth.

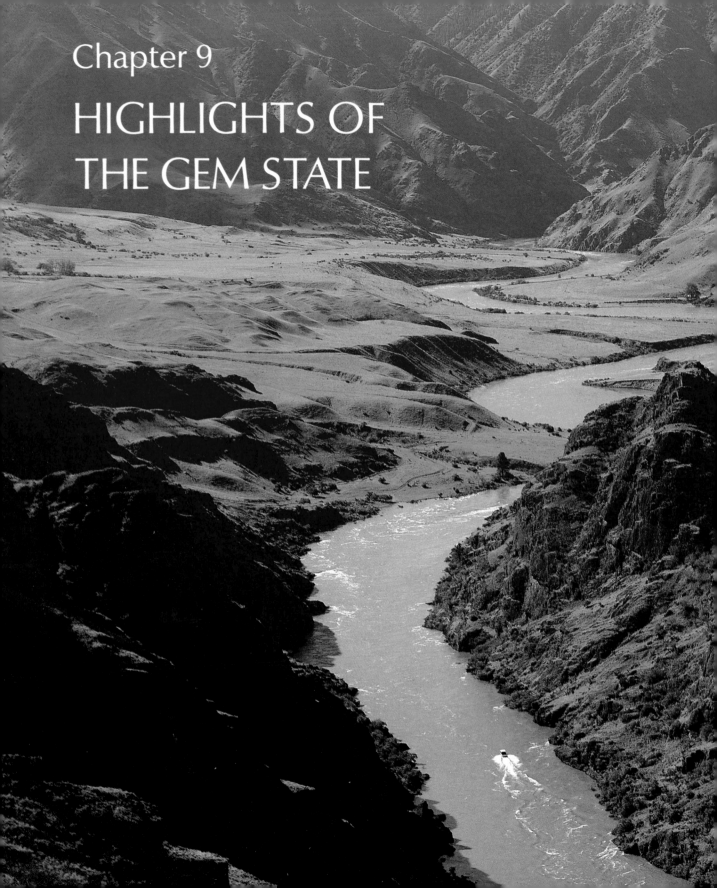

Chapter 9
HIGHLIGHTS OF THE GEM STATE

HIGHLIGHTS OF THE GEM STATE

The stunning diversity of Idaho's natural wonders, the vividness of its history, and the friendliness of its people lure thousands of visitors to the Gem State every year. A brief tour of Idaho, beginning at the Canadian border and moving southward, might include some of the following points of interest.

THE PANHANDLE

In Boundary County, the northernmost part of Idaho, nature reigns with timeless majesty. Near the logging town of Bonners Ferry, bird-watchers peer through binoculars at the many colorful species found at the Kootenai National Wildlife Refuge. Nearby, on the Moyie River, the water of fabulous Moyie Falls crashes between narrow canyon walls and rises in a sparkling mist.

Social and shopping activities keep visitors to Sandpoint, in Bonner County, busy throughout the year. This resort town on Lake Pend Oreille boasts the unusual Cedar Street Bridge, an arcade that stretches over a 350-foot (107-meter) creek and contains art galleries, crafts shops, stores, and eateries. The contents of Sandpoint's Vintage Wheel Museum are of great interest to people curious about the history of wheeled transportation. Sandpoint's annual music festivals fill summer nights with delightful melodies. Sleigh rides and snow sculptures are highlights of Sandpoint's winter carnivals.

Waterskiing, sailing, and strolling on the floating boardwalk are among the many pastimes that draw vacationers to the resort city

**The marina at Bayview
on Lake Pend Oreille**

of Coeur d'Alene on Coeur d'Alene Lake. Hopeful anglers try
their luck during the "Big One" Chinook salmon fishing contest,
held there each August. A century ago, steamboats plowed across
Coeur d'Alene Lake's deep waters. Today, visitors explore the lake
on the *Mish-an-Nock* and other cruise boats. History buffs who
want to learn more about Coeur d'Alene's exciting steamboat era
can view exhibits at the Museum of North Idaho.

Founded as a military outpost in 1878, Old Fort Sherman still
stands on the grounds of Coeur d'Alene's North Idaho College.
Those who wish to learn about the culture of the Coeur d'Alene
Indians can travel to nearby Worley on the Coeur d'Alene Indian
Reservation, where a festival is held every July.

The citizens of Wallace, in Shoshone County, often remind
visitors that the great forest fire of 1910 burned down one-third of

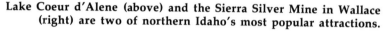
Lake Coeur d'Alene (above) and the Sierra Silver Mine in Wallace (right) are two of northern Idaho's most popular attractions.

their town. Mount Pulaski, a 5,480-foot (1,670-meter) peak visible from Wallace, was named in honor of forest ranger Ed Pulaski, who saved the lives of his fire-fighting crew during the blaze. Trapped by the flames, Pulaski hurried some forty men into an abandoned mining tunnel. "Finally, as the air outside became clearer," Pulaski afterwards recalled, "we were able to stagger to our feet and head for Wallace. . . . Shoes were burned off our feet and our clothing was in parched rags." Pulaski's heroism has earned him a special place in the hearts of Idahoans.

The Coeur d'Alene District Mining Museum stands in Wallace. Its collection of photographs, tools, and artifacts tells much about the region's silver-mining heritage. Perhaps even more interesting is a trip down into the old Sierra Silver Mine. Deep within, adventuresome tourists experience what it must have been like to be a miner a century ago. Mullan, Osburn, and Pinehurst all owe their existence to silver mining. Kellogg citizens claim laughingly that a jackass founded their town in 1885. Legend has it that the glittering outcropping of silver on which the famous Bunker Hill Mine was born was discovered when the mule of prospector Noah Kellogg kicked up some paydirt.

In Heyburn State Park, summer campers swim and fish on mountain lakes. Winter visitors steer ice boats or skate across the frozen ice. Heyburn is the largest and oldest state park in Idaho. One of the most unusual aspects of the park is the annual wild-rice harvest in the fall. Other lovely state parks in the Panhandle region include Priest Lake, Round Lake, and Farragut.

A visitor to Moscow, in Latah County's fertile Palouse Hills, exclaimed in the 1800s, "[It is] just a lane between two farms with a flax field on one side and a post office on the other." The establishment of the University of Idaho in 1889 soon changed that. While cultural and educational activities on the 450-acre (182-hectare) campus dominate town life, successful agricultural and commercial enterprises also attract new citizens to Moscow each year.

THE CENTRAL WILDERNESS

From mountaintop lookout stations, forest rangers scan Idaho's forest wilderness. Like lonely eagles, ranger pilots fly their single-engine planes over remote valleys to make sure that all is safe and peaceful. The vast wilderness lands of central Idaho stretch from the Clearwater River south to the north edge of the Snake River Plain. They include the Selway Bitterroot Wilderness, the Frank Church River of No Return Wilderness Area, and the Gospel-Hump Wilderness. Along wooded trails, skilled outfitters guide backpackers to spectacular campsites and superb hunting regions. In the Clearwater National Forest, camas bulbs still bloom on the Weippe Prairie. The Nez Perce National Forest, Payette National

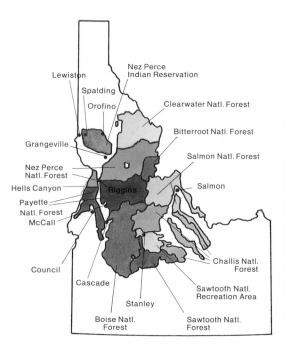

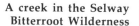

**A creek in the Selway
Bitterroot Wilderness**

Forest, Salmon National Forest, and Challis National Forest all offer beautiful sights that leave horseback riders, mountain climbers, and picnickers speechless.

The Nez Perce National Historical Park at Spalding draws visitors to the Nez Perce Indian Reservation. The Nez Perce National Historical Park Museum there has one of the nation's best collections of Nez Perce artifacts. The town of Orofino, located on reservation land, hosts the Clearwater County Fair and Lumberjack Days each September. Grinning crowds watch men and women saw and chop logs in exciting traditional logging competitions. Lewiston, Idaho's inland seaport, lies west of the reservation. Lewiston's fragrant Dogwood Festival brings vacationers to the region every spring.

Few travelers ever forget the stark wonder of Hells Canyon, North America's deepest canyon. Along the Idaho-Oregon border,

The Ore-Ida
Women's Challenge
bicycle race

the Snake River gorge twists and turns for 50 breathtaking miles
(80 kilometers). Measuring 7,900 feet (2,408 meters) in places, the
basalt cliffs of the Seven Devils Mountains form the eastern walls
of Hells Canyon. The gorgeous, panoramic view from Heaven's
Gate Lookout extends into four states: Washington, Oregon,
Idaho, and Montana.

McCall residents sometimes brag that their town offers Idaho's
best vacation opportunities. In the winter, skiers glide down
nearby Brundage Mountain. In the summer, boaters enjoy lovely
Payette Lake. In truth, though, almost every town in the Central
Wilderness region offers fun for visitors. In Grangeville, for
example, athletes gather every August to bicycle, swim, and run in
the Camas Prairie Triathlon. The course of the annual Ore-Ida
Women's Challenge bicycle race takes world-class competitors
through the awesome Sawtooth Mountains. In Riggins, kayaks
bob and jet boats zoom during annual Salmon River races.

Upriver, the town of Salmon calls itself the "White-water Capital of the World." On rubber rafts, excited vacationers paddle and shoot over falls and rapids on the fabled "River of No Return."

Visitors to the towns of Council and Cascade can watch commercial lumbering operations. Modern cranes haul logs into mills where great, buzzing saw blades cut them into boards.

The unsettling thrill of an earthquake shook Idahoans from Challis to Mackay and beyond on October 28, 1983. Measuring 7.3 on the Richter scale, the earth's violent shock lifted Borah Peak another foot (one-third of a meter) in height and sank Thousand Springs Valley 4 feet (1.2 meters). The resulting landslides, flooding, and property damage reminded people in the region how truly wild their state can be.

BOISE AND THE SOUTHWEST

The French Canadian trappers who first saw the lovely river lined with willows and cottonwoods called it *la riviere boise*, "the wooded river." When soldiers established a new fort on the river in 1863, they named it Boise. Today, Idaho's unique capital is often called the "City of Trees." Few cities in the United States so successfully combine the bustle of an urban business and cultural center with the beauty and excitement of the great outdoors.

Boise's chugging Tour Train is one fun way to view the city during the summer. One attraction of interest in the city is the Idaho State Capitol. Built with sandstone quarried from nearby Table Rock and completed in 1920, the handsome building recalls the classical style of the United States Capitol. The Idaho State Historical Museum, which includes such exhibits as an Old West saloon and a blacksmith's forge, also fascinates visitors. Perhaps even more engrossing is a tour of the Old Idaho Penitentiary,

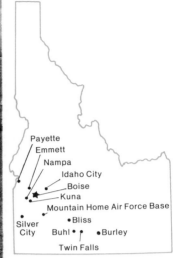

Boise, Idaho's capital city

located at the end of Warm Springs Avenue. For 103 years, until it closed in 1973, the "Old Pen" housed the state's worst criminals. The prison grounds also contain the Idaho Transportation Museum, Electricity Museum, and Printing Museum.

Music at the city Band Shell and theater presented at the annual Idaho Shakespeare Festival soothe Boise residents after sunset. Listening to concerts at Boise State University's Morrison Center for the Performing Arts or a stroll through the Boise Art Museum are also relaxing pastimes. In the Old Boise district, as well as at the Eighth Street Marketplace, people can shop in restored buildings of historic interest.

Boise's many parks, including C. W. Moore Park, Military Reserve Park, Julia Davis Park, and nearby Barber Park, provide places for fun or quiet reflection. Within the city limits, people can lazily float down the Boise River on inner tubes or cast their lines and fish for trout. Bigger animals can be viewed at the Boise City Zoo. Camels, tigers, and grizzly bears are among the one hundred species of wildlife found there. Children especially like scampering through the special petting zoo.

Left: The Snake River Birds of Prey Natural Area
Above: A family panning for gold near Idaho City

Within easy drives of Boise are a number of other Idaho attractions. Nature lovers never forget visiting the huge Snake River Birds of Prey Natural Area south of Kuna. It is argued that more eagles, hawks, and prairie falcons nest there than anywhere else in the world. Bird-watchers also enjoy the Lake Lowell Deer Flat National Wildlife Refuge near Nampa, where thousands of migratory ducks and geese gather each winter.

Along the Boise River west of Boise, fruit trees blossom in great fields of color. In towns such as Emmett and Payette, farmers often invite tourists to pick their own fresh apples and cherries. Roadside vegetable stands in the area entice people with their tasty produce.

Relics of Idaho's gold-rush era greet travelers who journey into the mountains northeast of Boise. Twenty-five thousand miners flocked into Idaho City in the 1860s, making it the largest city in the Northwest for a time. The bustling boomtown flavor of those

Rain-washed buildings from Idaho's mining-boom era still stand in historic Silver City, known as the "Queen of Idaho Ghost Towns."

exciting days remains there still. Visitors stride along the wooden boardwalks past saloons and general stores. At the Boot Hill Cemetery, headstones mark the graves of many long-gone miners. People who feel lucky can pan for gold in local creeks.

Most of Idaho's mining towns are merely ghost towns today. In the Boise Basin, dust blows through the streets of such deserted towns as Pioneerville, Placerville, and Quartzburg. The Gem State's best-preserved ghost town is Silver City, tucked away in the Owyhee Mountains southwest of Boise. Visitors walk among the rustic old buildings that housed the post office, newspaper, schoolhouse, and hotel, listening for echoes of the brawling mining days.

Thoughts of the past are quickly forgotten by visitors at the Mountain Home Air Force Base, home of the 366th Tactical Fighter Wing. During its September air show, F111A and EF-111A Raven fighter jets streak across the sky at wild speeds. At other times, tour groups at the base can learn about modern radar and communication techniques and see security-dog demonstrations.

Balanced Rock (left) and Bruneau Dunes State Park (right)

South of Mountain Home lies Bruneau Dunes State Park. Vacationers marvel at the quirks of nature as they climb some of America's highest sand dunes. Photographers can snap pictures of the unusual wildlife that exists in this desert setting. Farther south, the Bruneau River cuts through Bruneau Canyon. The desert flats here split suddenly in two, leaving a narrow gorge of spectacular depth and color.

In September 1844, emigrant Edward Parrish scribed in his diary, "We crossed the river safely after noon today and camped on a fine bed of grass within site of the ford." Today, visitors to Three Island Crossing State Park near Glenns Ferry may camp beside the same Snake River ford where so many settlers crossed on their journey along the Oregon Trail. Wagon-wheel ruts are still visible along the dusty path. Picnickers can examine the replica of a prairie schooner or gaze at the buffalo and longhorn cattle that graze in a nearby pasture.

To the east, near Bliss, lie the Hagerman Fossil Beds. Here scientists have excavated the skeletons of a prehistoric, zebralike horse known to zoologists as *Plesippus Shoshonensis*. Farther south, near Buhl, is the amazing, 40-foot-(12-meter-) high Balanced Rock, which seems to teeter with every breeze.

Visitors to Twin Falls can observe firsthand the power of the mighty Snake River. Nearby, the white waters of 212-foot-(65-meter-) high Shoshone Falls, the "Niagara of the West," plunge spectacularly. A drive across nearby Perrine Bridge provides fantastic Snake River views as well. Not far from the bridge, daredevil Evel Knievel made headlines in 1974. He unsuccessfully attempted to jump the mile-wide canyon in a jet-powered "skycycle"—and lived to tell about it. Daredevils today might prefer to join in the speedboat races of the annual Burley Regatta, held farther up the river, at Burley.

THE SOUTHEAST

Cool dark caves, tall pillarlike rocks, stony river gorges, and plains of lava ash mark the lands of southeastern Idaho. The hand of nature seems to have performed many unusual experiments there. In Lincoln County north of Shoshone, the Mammoth Cave and the Shoshone Ice Cave both stretch deep beneath the desert floor. Farther east, near American Falls, is the Crystal Ice Cave. Here, visitors descend 155 feet (47 meters) into the heart of a dead volcano where trickling water freezes into odd ice formations. Cave explorers who enter the Minnetonka Cave, a limestone cave near Bear Lake, walk along a winding trail through rooms of wondrous stalagmites and stalactites.

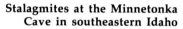

Stalagmites at the Minnetonka Cave in southeastern Idaho

The map shows the following locations: Targhee Natl. Forest, Rexburg, Idaho Falls, Arco, Blackfoot, Craters of the Moon Natl. Monument, Fort Hall Indian Reservation, Shoshone, American Falls, Silent City of Rocks, Malad City, Preston, Driggs, Pocatello, Caribou Natl. Forest, Paris, Cache Natl. Forest.

One of Idaho's most famous landmarks is the Craters of the Moon National Monument, southwest of Arco. On a plain of ancient volcanic lava, jutting cinder buttes, coal-black spatter cones, and twisting lava tubes have left the earth resembling the surface of the moon.

At the Silent City of Rocks, outside of Almo, huge granite columns—some thrusting sixty stories into the sky—have astonished travelers for decades. "We were so spellbound with the beauty and strangeness of it all," declared one early traveler on the nearby California Trail, "that no thought of Indians entered our head." Nineteenth-century pioneers literally left their mark on Register Rock at Massacre Rocks State Park in Power County. As early as 1849, travelers on the Oregon Trail stopped there and autographed the boulder with paint, tar, or axle grease.

The junction of several busy railroads won Pocatello the nickname "Gate City." Today, tourists can walk into the old Oregon Short Line Depot or the Bannock County Historical Museum and recapture the feeling of the city's railroad heritage.

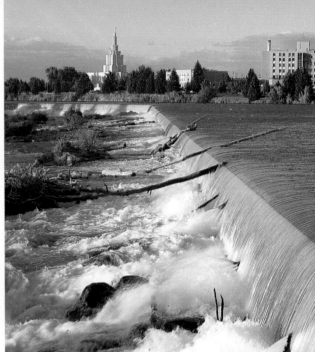

Craters of the Moon National Monument (left) lies west of Idaho Falls (right).

The Idaho Museum of Natural History, on the Idaho State University campus, has preserved many fascinating relics of Indian and pioneering days. The replica of old Fort Hall near the edge of town lets visitors step back in time into Idaho's fur trapping era. North and west of Pocatello, travelers can browse through Shoshone-Bannock trading posts and buy authentic native arts and crafts on the Fort Hall Indian Reservation.

Rodeos in Blackfoot, Pioneer Day celebrations in Idaho Falls, the International Folk Dance festival in Rexburg, and hot-air balloon races in Driggs all draw enthusiastic crowds to southeastern Idaho each year. In the area near the Utah border, the state's Mormon history is still evident. In such towns as Preston, Paris, Malad City, Montpelier, and Soda Springs, carefully planned streets and quaint homes reveal the lasting Mormon values of organization and community spirit. The Mormon churches and tabernacles found here often display handsome architectural designs.

Huge granite rocks pierce the landscape at the Silent City of Rocks near Almo.

On the outskirts of Rigby in Jefferson County, a sign reads,
"Welcome to Rigby—Birthplace of T.V." In the 1920s, a brilliant
young teenager named Philo T. Farnsworth first sketched his
ideas for an "image dissector tube" on the blackboard of a
chemistry classroom at Rigby Senior High School. As an adult
living in Utah, Farnsworth pursued his dream. His tube became
instrumental in the invention of television.

Wilderness adventure awaits vacationers along the Idaho-
Wyoming border. In the desert lands north of St. Anthony, the
St. Anthony Dunes stretch for 35 miles (56 kilometers). Visitors
walk among the wind-swept sands or speed along trails in dune
buggies. Campers and picnickers relax at sites in the vast Targhee,
Cache, and Caribou national forests. Harriman State Park and
Henry's Lake State Park are especially popular. Henry's Fork of
the Snake River offers some of the world's best fly fishing. The
river roars with unmatched grandeur at Lower Mesa Falls and
Upper Mesa Falls.

Upper Mesa
Falls on the
Snake River

As a young boy in the 1920s, writer Wallace Stegner camped
with his family beside the Upper Mesa Falls and never forgot the
experience. "I gave my heart to the mountains," he later recalled,
"the minute I stood beside this river with its spray in my face and
watched it thunder into foam, smooth to green glass over sunken
rocks, shatter to foam again. I was fascinated by how it sped by
and yet was always there; its roar shook both the earth and
me. . . . By such a river it is impossible to believe that one will ever
be tired or old."

The state of Idaho both starts and ends with its mountains and
rivers. They give and nurture life in beautiful and challenging
combinations. The people who draw upon this land for their
livelihood and inspiration can truly claim that Idaho is the "Gem
State" of America.

FACTS AT A GLANCE

GENERAL INFORMATION

Statehood: July 3, 1890, forty-third state

Origin of Name: The word *Idaho* was invented by George M. Willing. In 1860, Willing tried to convince Congress to adopt the name *Idaho* for the new territory of the Pikes Peak region, saying that it meant "gem of the mountains" in an Indian language. Congress discovered that *Idaho* was an invented word, however, and decided to call the new territory *Colorado* instead. In 1863, when a territory was being formed from the region that makes up all of present-day Idaho and Montana and most of Wyoming, the name *Idaho* was again suggested. This time, Congress agreed to the name.

State Capital: Boise

State Nickname: Gem State

State Flag: Idaho's flag consists of the state seal on a blue field. The woman on the seal holding a scale and a spear symbolizes liberty, justice, and equality. A miner represents mineral resources. An elk's head symbolizes wildlife. A pine tree represents forests. A sheaf of grain represents agriculture. The seal also contains the state motto. A circle with "Great Seal of the State of Idaho" in black letters on a gold background surrounds the seal. Below the seal is a gold scroll with "State of Idaho" in gold letters on a red background.

State Motto: *Esto perpetua*; Latin words meaning "It is forever"

State Flower: Syringa

State Tree: Western white pine

State Bird: Mountain bluebird

State Horse: Appaloosa

State Gem: Star garnet

State Song: "Here We Have Idaho," adopted in 1931, words by McKinley Helm and Albert J. Tompkins, music by Sallie Hume-Douglas:

And here we have Idaho,
Winning her way to fame.
Silver and gold in the sunlight blaze,
And romance lies in her name;
Singing, we're singing of you, ah, proudly, too;
All our lives through we'll go singing,
Singing of you, Alma mater, our Idaho.

POPULATION

Population: 944,038, forty-first among the states (1980 census)

Population Density: 11 people per sq. mi. (4 people per km²)

Population Distribution: Sixty percent of Idaho's people live in cities or towns. More than one-sixth of Idaho's population live in or near Boise, the state's largest city. The southern region contains many more people than the thinly populated northern Panhandle.

Boise	102,160
Pocatello	46,340
Idaho Falls	39,734
Lewiston	27,986
Twin Falls	26,209
Nampa	25,112
Coeur d'Alene	20,054
Caldwell	17,699
Moscow	16,513
Rexburg	11,559

Population Growth: Idaho was one of the last United States areas to be settled, and the only state over which no other nation's flag has ever flown. For many years, it was one of America's least-populated territories. After an 1860 gold rush, Idaho's population began to grow. Farmers, miners, and lumbermen contributed to a sharp rise in population between 1880 and 1920. Growth was again rapid after 1960. Since then, Idaho's economic growth and physical attractions have made it one of the fastest-growing states in the nation.

Year	Population
1870	14,999
1880	32,610
1890	88,548
1900	161,772

```
1910  . . . . . . . . . . . . . . . . . . . . . . . . . . . . . . . . . . . . . . . . . . . . . . . . .  325,594
1920  . . . . . . . . . . . . . . . . . . . . . . . . . . . . . . . . . . . . . . . . . . . . . . . . .  431,886
1930  . . . . . . . . . . . . . . . . . . . . . . . . . . . . . . . . . . . . . . . . . . . . . . . . .  445,032
1940  . . . . . . . . . . . . . . . . . . . . . . . . . . . . . . . . . . . . . . . . . . . . . . . . .  524,873
1950  . . . . . . . . . . . . . . . . . . . . . . . . . . . . . . . . . . . . . . . . . . . . . . . . .  588,637
1960  . . . . . . . . . . . . . . . . . . . . . . . . . . . . . . . . . . . . . . . . . . . . . . . . .  667,191
1970  . . . . . . . . . . . . . . . . . . . . . . . . . . . . . . . . . . . . . . . . . . . . . . . . .  713,015
1980  . . . . . . . . . . . . . . . . . . . . . . . . . . . . . . . . . . . . . . . . . . . . . . . . .  944,038
```

GEOGRAPHY

Borders: Idaho is bordered by Montana and Wyoming on the east, Utah and Nevada on the south, and Oregon and Washington on the west. The Canadian province of British Columbia borders Idaho on the north.

Highest Point: Borah Peak, 12,662 ft. (3,859 m)

Lowest Point: Snake River at Lewiston, 710 ft. (216 m)

Greatest Distances: North to south—483 mi. (777 km)
East to west—316 mi. (509 km)

Area: 83,564 sq. mi. (216,431 km²)

Rank in Area Among the States: Thirteenth

National Forests and Parklands: Forests cover more than 40 percent of Idaho. Densely wooded land, rugged mountains, and other natural wonders combine to give the state miles of parkland. Idaho contains three national parks and monuments: Craters of the Moon National Monument, Nez Perce National Historical Park, and part of Yellowstone National Park. Idaho also has fifteen national forests: Bitterroot, Boise, Cache, Caribou, Challis, Clearwater, Coeur d'Alene, Kaniksu, Kootenai, Nez Perce, Payette, St. Joe, Salmon, Sawtooth, and Targhee. In central Idaho, the Selway Bitterroot Wilderness, the Frank Church River of No Return Wilderness Area, and the Gospel-Hump Wilderness area combine to make up the nation's largest and least-explored wilderness area.

Rivers: Melting snows from Idaho's many rugged mountains provide water for dozens of fast-moving rivers. Idaho has more than 16,000 mi. (25,749 km) of rivers and streams, one of the largest totals of any state. Most of the state lies west of the Continental Divide. Consequently, the waters of most of the state's streams and rivers eventually find their way to the Pacific Ocean. Only one major river, the Great Bear, flows southeast. It empties into Utah's Great Salt Lake.

Idaho's most majestic river, the Snake, begins at Yellowstone National Park in Wyoming and flows across the southern and western portions of the state before flowing into the Columbia River. Most of the Snake River's 1,038-mi. (1,671-km)

The town of Stanley lies in the Sawtooth National Recreation Area.

journey occurs within Idaho's borders. The Clearwater River and the ferocious Salmon River, both of which are branches of the Snake River, are located entirely within the state. The Big Wood, Blackfoot, Payette, Weiser, and Boise are other branches of the Snake. Two other rivers, the Big Lost River and Little Lost River, simply disappear in Butte County. In the northern part of the state, the Kootenai, Pend Oreille, and Spokane rivers all eventually flow into the Columbia River. The St. Joe, St. Maries, and Coeur d'Alene, also in the north, served as lumber routes.

Lakes: Mountain upheavals and glacial action have blessed Idaho with more than two thousand natural lakes. These vary in size from small ponds to 148-sq.-mi. (383-km^2) Lake Pend Oreille in the far northern part of the state. Other large natural lakes include Coeur d'Alene Lake, Priest Lake, and Hayden Lake, in the north; Payette Lake, in the central part of the state; Henry's Lake, near the Wyoming border; and Bear Lake, on the Idaho-Utah border. Dams have formed eleven man-made lakes on the Snake River, including the American Falls, Palisades, Blackfoot River, Anderson Ranch, Lucky Peak, Cascade, and Dworshak reservoirs.

Winter scene, Sun Valley

Topography: Idaho contains four major topographical regions: the Northern Rocky Mountains, Middle Rocky Mountains, Columbia Plateau, and Basin and Range. The Northern Rocky Mountains region, which covers most of the northern Panhandle and reaches down into central Idaho, has some of the roughest mountains and wilderness land in the United States. The land is characterized by huge peaks, many of them over 10,000 ft. (3,048 m), separated by deep canyons and gorges. In this region, the U.S. Forest Service has designated several "primitive areas" that are preserved without roads or other modern improvements. The area known as the Central Wilderness, bordered on the west by the Seven Devils Mountains and the east by the Bitterroots, is some of the most inaccessible land in the country.

The Middle Rocky Mountains form a belt 10 to 35 mi. (16 to 56 km) wide along the Idaho-Wyoming border. This area has eight mountain ranges, with peaks ranging from 7,000 to 10,000 ft. (2,134 to 3,048 m).

The Columbia Plateau includes southwest Idaho and a section of land along the western edge of the northern Panhandle. It is a region of fertile plateaus and valleys. The Snake River Plain cuts through the plateau in the southern part of the state. The Columbia Plateau, especially areas irrigated by the Snake River, has the state's best farmland.

The Basin and Range region lies wedged between the Columbia Plateau and the Middle Rocky Mountains in the state's southeastern corner. It contains deep valleys and grassy plateaus separated by many small mountain ranges. Sheep graze in this dry region.

Climate: Idaho's climate is fairly temperate in comparison to some surrounding states. Warm, moist winds from the Pacific Ocean tend to warm the northern third of the state. Also, the mountains along the eastern part of Idaho tend to hold back

Wildflowers such as dwarf buckwheat and Anderson's larkspurs (above) and trees such as lodgepole pines (right) are among the many kinds of plants found in Idaho.

cold winter winds from the north and east. However, frigid temperatures can occur in the mountainous areas.

Differences in elevation cause temperatures to vary across the state. Temperatures in Boise and Lewiston average 75° F. (24° C) in July, while in cooler Coeur d'Alene and Idaho Falls, the average July temperature is 70° F. (21° C). In January, Lewiston's temperature averages 30° F. (-1° C). The average January temperature in Boise and Coeur d'Alene is 27° F. (-3° C). Idaho Falls residents shiver with average January temperatures of 16° F. (-9° C).

Precipitation also differs throughout the state. The land along the Snake River Plain receives less than 10 in. (25 cm) per year. Mountainous regions in the central part of the state and in the northern Panhandle receive about 32 in. (81 cm) annually. The highest mountains may receive as much as 200 in. (508 cm) of snow per year.

NATURE

Trees: White pine, Douglas fir, white fir, lodgepole pine, ponderosa pine, spruce, larch, birch, willow, aspen, hemlock, cedar, mountain ash, cottonwood

Wild Plants: Snowberry, chokecherry, huckleberry, wheatgrass, fescue, syringa, sagebrush, greasewood, cheatgrass, mountain heath, rabbitbrush, dogwood, snowberry, thimbleberry, stonecup, mariposa lily, prickly pear, Indian paintbrush, hollyhock, skunk cabbage

114

Animals: Moose, elk, chipmunks, squirrels, porcupines, beavers, deer, lynxes, cougars, black bears, grizzly bears, mountain goats, buffalo, prairie dogs, marmots, deer mice, badgers, pronghorn antelopes, bighorn sheep, jackrabbits, voles, horned toads, rattlesnakes, whiptailed lizards, bobcats, coyotes, minks, otters, raccoons, foxes, cottontail rabbits

Birds: Ducks, blue herons, hummingbirds, mountain bluebirds, bald eagles, western tanagers, Canada geese, trumpeter swans, golden eagles, red-tailed hawks, prairie chickens, prairie falcons, partridges, pheasants

Fish: Steelhead trout, rainbow trout, Kamloops trout, Dolly Varden trout, sturgeon, salmon, bass, perch, crappies, bluegill, catfish, grayling

GOVERNMENT

Idaho's constitution, adopted in 1889, has been amended more than one hundred times. Like the federal government, Idaho's government is divided into three branches. The legislative branch makes laws and assists the governor. It consists of a 42-member senate and an 84-member house of representatives. Legislators are elected for two-year terms.

The executive branch enforces the laws. The governor is elected to a four-year term and may serve an unlimited number of terms. The governor controls state spending, oversees the operation of state agencies, and is the state's chief law-enforcement officer. Voters elect a lieutenant governor, treasurer, secretary of state, attorney general, auditor, and superintendent of public instruction.

Courts make up the judicial branch. The highest court is the Idaho Supreme Court, which consists of a chief justice and four associate justices. Each of these justices is elected to a six-year term. Below the supreme court is the court of appeals. Its three justices also serve six-year terms. The justices of the state's district courts serve four-year terms. Each county also has magistrates, who serve four-year terms.

Sugar beets piled outside a processing plant in Nampa

Number of Counties: 44, plus a small part of Yellowstone National Park

U.S. Representatives: 2

Electoral Votes: 4

Voting Qualifications: U.S. citizen, at least eighteen years of age, resident of Idaho at least thirty days

EDUCATION

Even the most rugged pioneers in Idaho cared about the education of their children. Since the earliest days, schools have played an important role in Idaho. The first schools were Indian schools run by missionaries. In 1864, the territory established a common school system and provided a superintendent of territorial education. An 1887 law required school attendance through fifth grade. Today, all Idaho children between the ages of seven and fifteen are required to attend school.

Four state colleges serve Idaho. They are the University of Idaho at Moscow, Idaho State University at Pocatello, Lewis-Clark State College at Lewiston, and Boise State University at Boise. The state also runs two junior colleges: North Idaho Junior College at Coeur d'Alene, and College of Southern Idaho at Twin Falls. Three private colleges are church-affiliated. College of Idaho at Caldwell was founded by the Presbyterian church. Northwest Nazarene College at Nampa is affiliated with the Church of the Nazarene. The Mormon church operates Ricks College, a junior college at Rexburg.

Vacationers in the Lake Coeur d'Alene area

ECONOMY AND INDUSTRY

Principal Products:

Agriculture: Potatoes, beef cattle, hogs, wheat, oats, barley, hops, hay, sheep, dairy products, sugar beets, poultry, mint, dry beans, onions, dried peas, lentils, sweet corn, alfalfa, plums, cherries, apples, peaches, trout

Manufacturing: Food processing, lumber and wood products, chemicals, electronic equipment, nonelectrical machinery, rubber, plastic, metal items

Natural Resources: Silver, lead, copper, zinc, mercury, thorium, uranium, silica, tungsten, phosphate, vanadium, cadmium, molybdenum, gold, iron, clay, coal, soil, sand, gravel, limestone, water, semiprecious stones, forest products

Business and Trade: Service industries make up the largest percentage of Idaho's gross state product. The service industries that contribute the most to the state's economy include retail trade; wholesale trade of Idaho's forest, farm, and mineral products; government; and tourism-related services. Tourism has boomed in recent years, and now ranks third among Idaho industries.

Cities in other states have served as trade centers for Idaho goods. Salt Lake City, Utah, handles much of the trade of southeast Idaho. Spokane, Washington, serves the northern part of the state. Major Idaho trade centers include Lewiston, Boise, Nampa-Caldwell, Twin Falls, Pocatello, and Idaho Falls.

Manufacturing is the state's second-most-important economic activity. Food processing ranks first, followed by the manufacture of wood and lumber products and nonelectrical machinery. Idaho is also a leading mining state. It ranks first in the nation in silver production and second in lead.

Idaho produces one-fourth of the nation's potatoes. Idaho also leads the nation in commercial trout production. Idaho ranks second in the nation in production of lentils, barley, alfalfa, and dry edible peas; third in mint, Kentucky bluegrass, hops, and sugar beets; and fourth in onions.

Communication: Miners and prospectors read copies of Lewiston's *Golden News* when it appeared in 1862 as Idaho's first newspaper. Today, thousands of Idahoans read the eleven dailies and some fifty weeklies published in the state. Boise citizens have been buying copies of the *Idaho Statesman* since 1864. Other major Idaho dailies include the *Post-Register* of Idaho Falls, The Coeur d'Alene *Press*, the Lewiston *Tribune*, the *Times-News* of Twin Falls, and Pocatello's *Idaho State Journal*.

KFAU (now KIDO) of Boise began operating in 1922 as Idaho's first radio station. KIDO (now KTVB) of Boise went on the air in 1953 as the state's first television station. Today, Idaho has about twelve television stations and ninety radio stations.

Transportation: Early travel in Idaho was difficult because of the treacherous mountains. Even so, Idaho lay along the path of the famous Oregon Trail, and westbound travelers passed through the region before reaching the Pacific coast.

Today, four interstate highways serve Idaho. In the south, Interstate 84 enters the state near Payette and runs southeast to the Utah border. Interstate 86 branches off from Interstate 84 in Cassia County and travels to a junction near Pocatello. Here it meets Interstate 15, a north-south route that runs from the Utah border to the Montana border. Interstate 90 carries east-west traffic across the northern Panhandle. U.S. Highway 95, which runs along the western part of the state up to the Canadian border, is the state's main north-south highway. In all, some 63,000 mi. (101,386 km) of roads thread through Idaho's mountains, valleys, and plains.

Railroad tracks were first laid in Idaho in 1874. Today, two major commercial railroads run on about 2,000 mi. (3,219 km) of track. Freight operations are centered in Pocatello. Five Idaho cities have passenger lines. Idaho also has about 190 airports, including major airports in Boise, Idaho Falls, Pocatello, Lewiston, and Twin Falls.

A canal finished in 1975 made Lewiston an inland port. Grain and other products are transported along the canal and then the Columbia River to Portland, Oregon, and the Pacific Ocean.

SOCIAL AND CULTURAL LIFE

Museums: Idaho's rich Indian, pioneer, and mining heritage is preserved in the state's many museums. The Idaho Historical Museum in Boise, for example, has an Old West saloon, blacksmith's forge, turn-of-the-century kitchen, and Chinese apothecary. The Coeur d'Alene District Mining Museum in Wallace recalls the boom-and-bust days of the early miners. The Northern Pacific Depot Railroad Museum, also in Wallace, shows how railroads were integral to the development of the state. The Museum of North Idaho is a historical museum in Coeur d'Alene. St. Gertrude's Museum, in Cottonwood, features an impressive collection of Nez Perce artifacts. Boise's Basque Museum honors the largest Basque community outside of Europe. The Boise Basin Museum in Idaho City has rooms full of Old

Windsurfing (left) and skiing (right) are two of the many outdoor activities that can be enjoyed in Idaho.

West memorabilia. The Idaho Museum of Natural History in Pocatello has pioneer and Indian relics, as well as scale-model dinosaurs.

The Hemingway Western Studies Center in Boise features exhibits on art, literature, history, and archaeology. Boise also has museums of electricity and transportation. The Boise Art Museum features both traditional and contemporary works. Moscow boasts the University Gallery and Prichard Art Gallery.

Libraries: Idaho has about 125 public libraries. The University of Idaho Library, in Moscow, is the state's largest library. Other important libraries include the Idaho State Library and Idaho Supreme Court Library in Boise, the Idaho National Engineering Laboratory Technical Library in Idaho Falls, and the Idaho State Historical Library in Boise.

Performing Arts: Even though it has few large cities, Idaho boasts a lively cultural scene. Boise residents can enjoy the Boise Philharmonic, the American Festival Community Concerts, the Boise Little Theatre, and the annual Idaho Shakespeare Festival. The Morrison Center for the Performing Arts in Boise attracts top cultural events. Coeur d'Alene has such theater groups as the Carousel Players and the Coeur d'Alene Community Players. The Salmon River Playhouse entertains Salmon residents and tourists during the summertime. Moscow boasts two important dance groups, the American Festival Ballet Company and the Main Street Dance Company. Moscow and the University of Idaho also host the Washington-Idaho Symphony. The university city is also home to the Hartung Theatre and the Idaho Repertory Theatre. The Lewiston Civic Theatre offers a broad program of presentations. The famed National Oldtime Fiddlers Contest is a six-day event held every year in Weiser.

Sports and Recreation: Idaho is a paradise for lovers of the outdoors. Skiers flock to world-famous Sun Valley, as well as to such resorts as Bogus Basin, Schweitzer

Ski Basin, Pebble Creek, Brundage Mountain, and Grand Targhee. Idaho's spectacular and varied terrain can be enjoyed in the state's nineteen state parks and fifteen national forests, which offer opportunities for camping, boating, swimming, snowmobiling, hiking, backpacking, horseback riding, and hunting. Idaho is famous for its fishing. The state is also a mecca for white-water rafters. Many call the Salmon River the "white-water-rafting capital of the world." The Sawtooth National Recreation Area has scenic gorges, valleys, glacial basins, and more than 300 mi. (483 km) of trails. Proud Idahoans call it "America's Switzerland." Many Idahoans enjoy the rough-and-tumble sport of rodeo. Every year, Pocatello hosts the World Championship Cutter and Chariot Races.

Historic Sites and Landmarks:

Cataldo Mission, in Cataldo, is Idaho's oldest standing building. It was built, without benefit of nails, in the 1850s by Coeur d'Alene Indians under the direction of Jesuit missionaries.

Experimental Breeder Reactor #1, near Arco, was the first power plant in the world to produce electricity by using atomic energy. Visitors may tour the now-inoperative reactor, which has been designated a National Historic Landmark.

Fort Hall, in Pocatello, is a replica of a trading post that was founded by Nathaniel Wyeth in 1834 and became an important landmark along the Oregon Trail.

Ernest Hemingway Memorial, along Trail Creek near Sun Valley, honors the Nobel-Prizewinning author, who spent his final years in Idaho.

Idaho City, near Boise, is a restored 1860s mining town that produced more gold than Alaska.

Nez Perce National Historical Park and Museum, in Spalding, preserves the history and culture of the Nez Perce people.

Old Fort Boise, in Parma, is the exact replica of a trading post built in 1834.

Old Idaho Penitentiary, in Boise, is one of only four territorial prisons in the country still in existence. It served as the state prison for more than a hundred years.

Oregon Short Line Depot, in Pocatello, is a three-story building that served as a transportation hub at the turn of the century.

Silent City of Rocks, near Burley, is an area where huge granite columns rise up from the desert. Still visible on some of the rocks are inscriptions written in axle grease by pioneers who stopped while traveling along the California Trail.

The interior of the historic Cataldo Mission

Silver City, once a booming mining town, is now Idaho's best-preserved ghost town.

Wallace, a former mining town listed on the National Register of Historic Places, welcomes visitors to explore such historic sites as the Union Pacific Train Depot, the Smokehouse Building of 1890, and the Sierra Silver Mine.

Other Interesting Places to Visit:

Balanced Rock, near Castleford, is a mushroom-shaped rock that has become an Idaho landmark.

Borah Peak, near Mackay, is Idaho's highest peak.

Bruneau Dunes State Park, near Mountain Home, features magnificent sand dunes, the tallest of which towers 470 ft. (143 m).

Craters of the Moon National Monument, near Arco, is an eerie volcanic landscape featuring a variety of caves and craters.

Crystal Ice Cave, near American Falls, lies deep inside a dormant volcano and features a frozen lake, a frozen waterfall, and other beautiful ice formations.

Emerald Creek, near Clarkia, is one of the few sites in the world where star garnets can be found. Visitors are permitted to dig for the rare gems.

Borah Peak is Idaho's highest peak.

Fort Hall Indian Reservation, in southeastern Idaho, is the home of the Shoshone-Bannock Indians. Every August, they celebrate their culture and heritage with the Shoshone-Bannock Indian Festival and Rodeo.

Hells Canyon National Recreation Area, in southwestern Idaho, is the site of North America's deepest gorge.

Idaho State Capitol, in Boise, is the nation's only state capitol building heated with geothermal hot water.

Lava Hot Springs, near Pocatello, is a popular resort and spa that boasts natural mineral springs.

Minnetonka Cave, near St. Charles, is a huge sandstone cave that features dazzling ice-crystal walls and prehistoric fossils of plants and marine animals.

Moyie Falls, on the Moyie River near Bonners Ferry, are some of the most spectacular waterfalls in Idaho.

Shoshone Falls, near Shoshone, is nicknamed the "Niagara of the West." Its dazzling falls plunge more than 200 ft. (61 m).

Shoshone Ice Cave, near Shoshone, is a lava tube, spanning three blocks, in which flowing air currents have formed spectacular ice formations.

Sun Valley features some of the finest skiing in North America.

Soda Springs, in southeastern Idaho, is famous for its geyser, which spews mineral water more than 100 ft. (30 m) into the air.

Sun Valley, in central Idaho, is America's oldest ski resort and features some of the finest alpine skiing in North America.

Thousand Springs, in the Hagerman Valley, is where the disappearing Lost River of east-central Idaho bursts forth through black canyon cliffs above the Snake River.

World Center for Birds of Prey, near Boise, is a major site for the breeding of peregrine falcons.

World's Largest Trout Ranch, in Twin Falls, is a breeding ground for one of Idaho's major "crops."

IMPORTANT DATES

c. 13,500 B.C. — Earliest-known inhabitants of Idaho, in caves of Jerome County, create tools such as arrowheads and pottery

c. 1730 — Shoshone Indians acquire horses

1803 — United States buys Louisiana Territory, including part of present-day Idaho, from France

A Shoshone in traditional dress

1805—Members of the Lewis and Clark expedition become the first white men to set foot in Idaho

1809—David Thompson builds the Idaho region's first trading post, at Lake Pend Oreille

1810—Andrew Henry of the St. Louis Fur Company leads several hundred fur trappers into southeastern Idaho; they build Fort Henry in present-day Fremont County

1818—Donald MacKenzie of the North West Company begins leading fur-trapping expeditions into Idaho

1832—Fur trappers meet at Pierre's Hole for the largest trapper rendezvous ever held

1834—Fort Hall and Fort Boise are founded; Jason Lee performs the first Sunday service in the Idaho region

1836—Henry and Eliza Spalding found a mission at Lapwai and open the region's first Indian mission school

1841—First Oregon-bound wagon train crosses the Idaho territory

1843—A surveying party led by John C. Frémont crosses southern Idaho

1850—Construction of the Roman Catholic mission that becomes known as the Cataldo Mission begins

1855—Mormons begin settling in southern Idaho

1858—Conflicts with Indians cause Mormons to abandon their settlement at Lemhi

1860—Franklin, Idaho's first permanent white settlement, is founded; a party led by Elias D. Pierce discovers gold in the Clearwater River region

1862—Gold is discovered in the Boise Basin

1863—Idaho Territory, comprising all of present-day Idaho and Montana and most of Wyoming, is established by Congress; militia led by Colonel Patrick Connor massacres Shoshones in the Battle of Bear River, the worst slaughter of Indians in American history

1864—Territorial legislature votes to move the territorial capital from Lewiston to newly founded Boise; Congress forms Montana Territory, reducing the size of Idaho Territory

1868—Creation of Wyoming Territory further reduces the size of Idaho Territory, leaving it with the boundaries of the present-day state

1874—Northern Pacific and Union Pacific railroads build branch lines in Idaho

1877—Federal troops defeat Chief Joseph and the Nez Perce Indians in the Nez Perce War

1878—Soldiers rout Indians in the Bannock War

1880—Discovery of silver and lead deposits in the Wood River area attracts fortune hunters

1884—Prospectors find one of the world's richest silver deposits in Coeur d'Alene Mountains

1885—Test Oath Act prohibits all Mormons from voting

1889—Political leaders meet in Boise to write a state constitution; the legislature authorizes the establishment of the University of Idaho

1890—Idaho enters the Union as the forty-third state

1892—Violent labor disputes occur between union miners and mine owners in the Coeur d'Alene district; to end the strife, Governor N. B. Willey declares martial law

1894—Carey Act enables Idaho to begin many irrigation projects

These two photographs show a Coeur d'Alene mine before and after it was blown up by miners during labor disputes in 1892.

1896 — Mormons regain the right to vote

1899 — Governor Frank Steunenberg declares martial law in the Coeur d'Alene district after miners destroy the Bunker Hill and Sullivan mine

1904 — Work begins on the Snake River's Minidoka Dam

1905 — Former Governor Frank Steunenberg is killed by a bomb wired to the gate of his house

1907 — The Steunenberg murder trial attracts national attention; William S. Borah, who prosecuted the case and who would become Idaho's most famous senator, takes office in the U.S. Senate

1910 — A great fire in northern Idaho destroys thousands of acres and kills eighty-five persons

1914 — Idaho's Moses Alexander becomes the nation's first Jewish governor

1915 — Arrowrock Dam, the tallest dam in the world at the time, begins operation

1924 — Craters of the Moon National Monument is established

1936 — Sun Valley, the Rocky Mountains' first famous ski resort, opens

1938 — First paved highway connecting northern and southern Idaho opens

1942 — Some of the thousands of Japanese Americans living along the Pacific coast are sent to the Minidoka Relocation Center in Jerome County

1949 — The Atomic Energy Commission establishes the National Reactor Testing Station (later called the Idaho National Engineering Laboratory) near Arco

This photograph of the Lost River Range shows the fault line caused by the earthquake that hit the area in 1983.

1951 — Electricity is generated from atomic energy for the first time at a testing station near Idaho Falls

1955 — Arco becomes the first community in the world to receive its entire power supply from nuclear energy

1959 — Engineers complete Brownlee Dam, the first of three large hydroelectric-power-producing dams along the Snake River

1965 — Nez Perce National Historical Park is established

1972 — Sunshine mine fire kills ninety-one men

1974 — Daredevil Evel Knievel makes an unsuccessful attempt to jump over Snake River Canyon on a jet-powered motorcycle

1975 — Columbia-Snake River Inland Waterway opens, making Lewiston the farthest-inland seaport in the West

1976 — Teton River Dam bursts, spilling 80 billion gal. (303 billion l) of water

1978 — The National Wild and Scenic Rivers Act preserves thousands of acres of Idaho wilderness land

1983 — The largest American earthquake in twenty-four years has its epicenter near Challis

1987 — The state legislature passes the Terrorism Training Act, which prevents terrorist training campaigns that could lead to violence

1988 — Forest fires char more than 300,000 acres (121,407 hectares) of Idaho forests

1990 — Idaho celebrates its centennial

MOSES ALEXANDER

GUTZON BORGLUM

JIM BRIDGER

IMPORTANT PEOPLE

Moses Alexander (1853-1932), politician; governor of Idaho (1915-19); the nation's first Jewish governor

Cecil Andrus (1931-   ), politician; governor (1971-77, 1987-   ); as U.S. secretary of the interior (1977-81), created legislation to preserve much of Alaska's wilderness

Ezra Taft Benson (1899-   ), born in Whitney; politician, religious leader; U.S. secretary of agriculture (1953-61); president of Church of Jesus Christ of Latter-day Saints (1985-   )

Benjamin Louis Eulalie de Bonneville (1796-1878), army officer, explorer; traveled through Idaho in 1832 during an expedition through the Northwest; inspired Washington Irving's *The Adventures of Captain Bonneville*

William Edgar Borah (1865-1940), politician; one of Idaho's most important political figures; first earned fame as prosecutor in the Steunenberg murder trial; U.S. senator (1907-40); as senator, supported many progressive reforms; led successful fight to keep U.S. out of the League of Nations; supported many New Deal policies; chairman of Senate Foreign Relations Committee (1924-33)

Gutzon Borglum (1867-1941), born near Bear Lake; sculptor; carved the likenesses of George Washington, Thomas Jefferson, Abraham Lincoln, and Theodore Roosevelt into the side of Mount Rushmore in South Dakota; also sculpted the large marble head of Lincoln displayed in the U.S. Capitol

James (Jim) Bridger (1804-1881), mountain man; explored Idaho and led expeditions throughout the region; won respect for his knowledge of Indian ways and his storytelling skills

Carol Ryrie Brink (1895-1981), born in Moscow; author; wrote many books for children and young adults; won 1936 Newbery Medal for *Caddie Woodlawn*

Frank Church (1924-1984), born in Boise; politician; U.S. senator (1957-80); chairman of Senate Foreign Relations Committee (1979); leading proponent of preserving wilderness areas in Idaho; sponsored legislation to create Sawtooth National Recreation Area

FRANK CHURCH

William Clark (1770-1838), explorer; in 1804, was sent, with Meriwether Lewis, to explore the newly acquired Louisiana Purchase territory and find a route to the Pacific Ocean; their travels took them through the Idaho region in 1805

John Colter (1775?-1813), explorer; member of Lewis and Clark expedition; later returned to the Northwest and explored areas of present-day Idaho; first white man to see the lands that are now part of Yellowstone National Park

Fred T. Dubois (1851-1930), politician; led fight to secure Idaho statehood; U.S. senator (1891-97,1901-07)

Philo Taylor Farnsworth (1906-1971), engineer, inventor; at age sixteen, while living in Rigby, developed the image dissector, an invention that led to the creation of television

PHILO T. FARNSWORTH

Vardis Fisher (1895-1968), born in Annis; author; gave vivid descriptions of frontier Idaho in his many novels; noted works include *A Tale of Valor: a Novel of the Lewis and Clark Expedition, The Children of God,* and *Mountain Man;* wrote *Idaho Guide,* the model for a highly acclaimed series of books about the states that was sponsored by the Works Progress Administration

Mary Hallock Foote (1847-1938), author, illustrator; wrote stories about Idaho miners, dam builders, irrigators, and farmers; became acclaimed as "the dean of women illustrators"; wrote *Edith Bonham,* a semi-autobiographical novel

VARDIS FISHER

John C. Frémont (1813-1890), explorer and soldier; led an expedition that charted the most favorable route through the Rockies to Oregon; explored the Snake River region

Lawrence Henry Gipson (1880-1971), historian, educator; won acclaim for his eight-volume work, *The British Empire before the American Revolution;* taught for many years at colleges in Idaho

Emma Edwards Green (1856-1942), artist; designed Idaho's state seal, becoming the only woman to design a state seal

Robert Vail Hansberger (1920-   ), businessman; directed Boise Cascade Corporation, (1956-72); headed Boise's Futura Industries Corporation (1972-   )

Orval Hansen (1926-   ), born in Firth; lawyer, politician; U.S. representative (1969-75); known as a thoughtful and moderate congressman

William Averell Harriman (1891-1986), statesman, businessman; held a number of important diplomatic and cabinet posts; in 1936 founded Sun Valley, America's first ski resort

W. AVERELL HARRIMAN

JAMES HAWLEY

WALTER JOHNSON

CHIEF JOSEPH

MERIWETHER LEWIS

James H. Hawley (1847-1929), lawyer, politician, author; became known as ''the Great Old Man of Idaho''; wrote *History of Idaho, Gem of the Mountains*

Ernest Miller Hemingway (1899-1961), author; one of the twentieth century's most influential writers; won 1954 Nobel Prize for literature; gained fame for his strong, robust novels and his adventurous, ''macho'' lifestyle; finished the novel *For Whom the Bell Tolls* while visiting Idaho; spent his final years near Ketchum

Mariel Hemingway (1961-   ), born in Ketchum; actress; granddaughter of Ernest Hemingway; appeared in a number of films, including *Manhattan* and *Star 80*

Walter Perry ''Big Train'' Johnson (1887-1946), professional baseball player; grew up in Weiser; considered one of the greatest pitchers in baseball history; starred for twenty-one years with the Washington Senators; won more games (416) than any other pitcher in American League history; holds major-league record of 110 shut-outs; struck out 3,508 batters, a record that lasted more than fifty years; was one of the first five players elected to the Baseball Hall of Fame

Chief Joseph (1840?-1904), Nez Perce chief; refused to sign treaty that would have stripped Nez Perce tribe of their lands; during the Nez Perce War of 1877, fought valiantly in the Battle of White Bird Canyon; led 750 men, women, and children on a grueling, 1,800-mi. (2,900-km) retreat toward Canada before surrendering to U.S. forces

Harmon Clayton Killebrew (1936-   ), born in Payette; professional baseball player; clubbed 573 major-league home runs, making him fifth on the all-time list; led American League in homers six times and runs batted in three times; won 1969 American League Most Valuable Player award; led Minnesota Twins to three championships

Vernon Law (1930-   ), born in Meridian; professional baseball player; won 162 major league games with Pittsburgh Pirates plus two in 1960 World Series; won 20 games and Cy Young Award in 1960

Meriwether Lewis (1774-1809), explorer; in 1804, with William Clark, led first official U.S. expedition to Pacific Ocean; their travels took them through the Idaho region in 1805; brought back information about Indians, plants, animals, and minerals of newly purchased Louisiana territory

James McClure (1924-   ), born in Payette; politician; U.S. representative (1966-71); U.S. senator (1973-90); chairman of Senate's Energy and Natural Resources Committee for six years

William McConnell (1839-1925), legislator; U.S. senator (1890-91); governor (1893-97); fought for women's suffrage and irrigation laws; established two normal (teachers') schools

Harry Orchard (1866-1954), born Albert Horsley; labor organizer; helped dynamite Bunker Hill and Sullivan ore concentrations in 1899; assassinated former governor Frank Steunenberg in 1905

HARRY ORCHARD

Ira B. Perrine (1861-1947), developer, engineer; secured funds necessary to irrigate Idaho's dry lands; experimented with varieties of crops

Gracie Bowers Pfost (1906-1965), politician; first Idaho woman to serve as a U.S. representative (1953-63)

Elias Davidson Pierce (1823?-1897), miner; prospected in Idaho and Nevada; led a group that discovered gold in the Clearwater River region in 1860

Henry Plummer (?-1864), outlaw; terrorized Lewiston; formed a gang known as the Innocents; fled Lewiston but was lynched in Montana in 1864

GRACIE PFOST

Ezra Loomis Pound (1885-1972), born in Hailey; poet, critic, editor; leader of the Imagist movement of poetry; influenced many major twentieth-century writers; best known for his cycle *Cantos*, which deals with subjects ranging from aesthetics to economics and describes many civilizations

Marjorie Reynolds (1921-   ), born in Buhl; actress; starred in the film *Life of Riley*

Sacagawea (1784?-1884), thought to have been born near present-day Lemhi; interpreter; known as "Bird Woman"; member of the Shoshone tribe who was captured and sold to a Canadian trapper in 1800; accompanied Lewis and Clark expedition as an interpreter and guide; served as a liaison and peacemaker between members of the expedition and Indians

EZRA POUND

George Laird Shoup (1836-1904), miner, merchant, politician; governor of Idaho Territory (1889); first Idaho governor (1890); sponsored idea of secret ballot for state elections; one of Idaho's first U.S. senators (1890-1901)

Robert Smylie (1914-   ), politician; governor (1955-67); as governor, implemented construction of several dams to harness power to the Snake River

Rosalie Sorrels (1933-   ), born in Boise; singer, composer; exercised the power of a storyteller while breathing life into her songs; composed "White Clouds" and "Rosalie, You Can't Go Home Again"

Henry Harmon Spalding (1804?-1874), missionary; first permanent white settler in Idaho; founded Lapwai Mission; established Idaho's first church and first school; introduced printing and milling to Idaho

ROBERT SMYLIE

FRANK STEUNENBERG

LANA TURNER

Frank Steunenberg (1861-1905), politician; published *Caldwell Tribune*; member of Idaho Constitutional Convention; governor (1897-1901); declared martial law against Coeur d'Alene strikers; was assassinated four years after leaving office

James Floyd Stevens (1892-1971), author; lived in Idaho for a time; wrote *Paul Bunyan*, a compilation of tales about the legendary lumberjack

Edward A. (E. A.) Stevenson (1831-1895), politician; governor of Idaho Territory (1885-89); called for an Idaho constitutional convention in 1890, used his influence to dissuade President Grover Cleveland from dividing Idaho into more than one state

Ted Trueblood (1913-1982), born in Idaho; writer; gained national reputation as a contributor to *Field and Stream, Elks Magazine*, and *True*; received many Idaho and national honors for his work for conservation

Lana Turner (1920-   ), born in Wallace; actress; glamorous star who became known as "the sweater girl" because of her trademark sweaters; starred in such films as *We Who Are Young, The Postman Always Rings Twice, Cass Timberlane*, and *Peyton Place*

Lawrence Frank (Larry) Wilson (1938-   ), born in Rigby; professional football player; defensive back with St. Louis Cardinals (1960-72); twice intercepted three passes in one game; elected to Pro Football Hall of Fame (1971)

GOVERNORS

George L. Shoup	1890	Chase A. Clark	1941-1943
N. B. Willey	1891-1893	C. A. Bottolfsen	1943-1945
William J. McConnell	1893-1897	Charles C. Gossett	1945
Frank Steunenberg	1897-1901	Arnold Williams	1945-1947
Frank W. Hunt	1901-1903	C. A. Robins	1947-1951
John T. Morrison	1903-1905	Len B. Jordan	1951-1955
Frank R. Gooding	1905-1909	Robert E. Smylie	1955-1967
James H. Brady	1909-1911	Don Samuelson	1967-1971
James H. Hawley	1911-1913	Cecil D. Andrus	1971-1977
John M. Haines	1913-1915	John V. Evans	1977-1987
Moses Alexander	1915-1919	Cecil D. Andrus	1987-
D. W. Davis	1919-1923		
C. C. Moore	1923-1927		
H. C. Baldridge	1927-1931		
C. Ben Ross	1931-1937		
Barzilla W. Clark	1937-1939		
C. A. Bottolfsen	1939-1941		

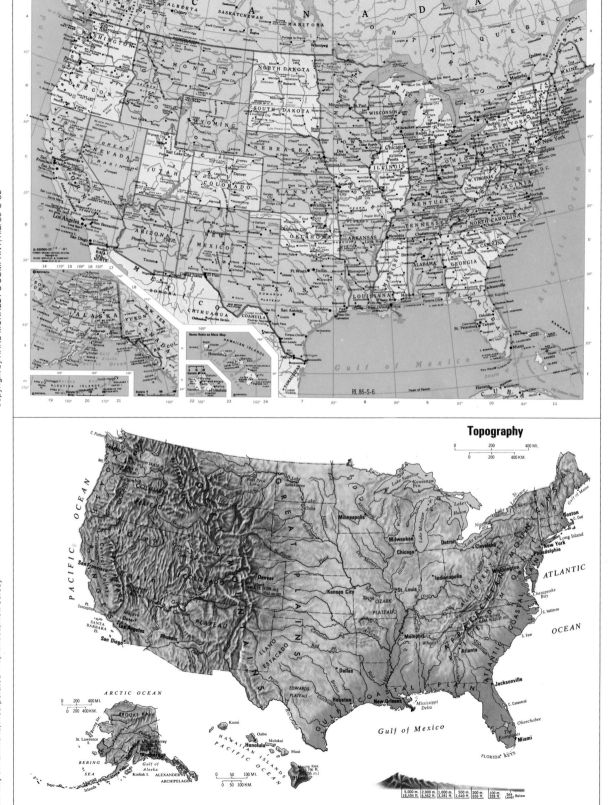

RL 86-S-6

Topography

5,000 m. | 2,000 m. | 1,000 m. | 500 m. | 200 m. | 100 m. | Sea
15,404 ft. | 6,562 ft. | 3,281 ft. | 1,640 ft. | 656 ft. | 328 ft. | Level
 | | | | | | Below

MAP KEY

Acequia	G5	Coeur d'Alene Indian Reservation	B2	Heyburn	G5	Parma	F2
Ahsahka	C2	Coeur d'Alene Lake	B2	Hill City	F3	Patterson	E5
Albion	G5	Coeur d'Alene Mountains	B2	Holbrook	G6	Paul	G5
Almo	G5	Coeur d'Alene River	B2	Hollister	G4	Payette	E2
American Falls	G6	Conda	G7	Homedale	F2	Payette Lake	E2
American Falls Dam	G5	Coolin	A2	Hope	A2	Payette River	F2
American Falls Reservoir	F5	Corral	F4	Horseshoe Bend	F2	Peck	C2
Ammon	F7	Cottonwood	C2	Howe	F6	Pend Oreille Lake	A2
Anderson Dam	F3	Council	E2	Humphrey	E6	Picabo	F4
Anderson Ranch Reservoir	F3	Craigmont	C2	Idaho City	F3	Pierce	C3
Arco	F5	Crane Creek Reservoir	E2	Idaho Falls	F6	Pinehurst	B2
Arimo	G6	Craters Lava Bed	F5	Indian Valley	E2	Pingree	F6
Arrowrock Reservoir	F3	Craters of the Moon National Monument	F5	Inkom	G6	Pioneer Mountains	F5
Ashton	E7	Crouch	E3	Iona	F7	Placerville	F3
Athol	B2	Culdesac	C2	Irwin	F7	Plummer	B2
Atlanta	F2	Dalton Gardens	B2	Island Park	E7	Pocatello	G6
Atomic City	F6	Dayton	G6	Island Park Reservoir	E7	Pollock	D2
Avery	B3	Deadwood Reservoir	E3	Jerome	G4	Ponderay	A2
Bancroft	G7	Deary	C2	Juliaetta	C2	Porthill	A2
Banks	E2	Declo	G5	Kamiah	C2	Post Falls	B2
Bannock Peak	G6	Deep Creek Mountains	G6	Kellogg	B2	Potlatch	C2
Bannock Range	G6	Desmet	B2	Kendrick	C2	Preston	G7
Basalt	F6	Diamond Peak	E5	Ketchum	F4	Priest Lake	A2
Bayview	B2	Dietrich	G4	Keuterville	C2	Priest River	A2
Bear Lake	G7	Donnelly	E2	Kimberly	G4	Princeton	C2
Bear River	G7	Dover	A2	King Hill	F3	Raft River	G5
Bellevue	F4	Downey	G7	Kingston	B3	Rathdrum	B2
Bennington	G7	Driggs	F7	Kooskia	C3	Rexburg	F7
Big Creek	D3	Drummond	F7	Kootenai River	A2	Richfield	F4
Big Creek Peak	E5	Dubois	E6	Kuna	F2	Riddle	G2
Big Lost River	F5	Dworshak Reservoir	C3	Laclede	A2	Rigby	F7
Big Southern Butte	F5	Eagle	F2	Lake Fork	E2	Riggins	D2
Big Wood River	F4	Eastport	A2	Lakeview	A2	Ririe	F7
Bitterroot Range	B3	Eden	G4	Lapwai	C2	Roberts	F6
Blackfoot	F6	Elba	G5	Lava Beds	F4	Rockland	G6
Blackfoot Mountains	F7	Elk City	D3	Lava Hot Springs	G6	Rogerson	G4
Blackfoot Reservoir	A2	Elk River	C2	Leadore	E5	Roswell	F2
Blanchard	A2	Ellis	E4	Lemhi	E5	Rupert	G5
Bliss	G4	Emida	B2	Lemhi Pass	E5	Sagle	A2
Bloomington	G7	Emmett	F2	Lemhi Range	E5	Salmon	D5
Boise	F2	Fairfield	F4	Lemhi River	E5	Salmon Creek Reservoir	G4
Boise River	F2	Fairview	G7	Lenore	C2	Salmon Falls Creek	G4
Bonners Ferry	A2	Felt	F7	Leslie	F5	Salmon River	D3
Borah Peak	E5	Fenn	D2	Letha	F2	Salmon River Mountains	D3
Bovill	C2	Ferdinand	C2	Lewiston	C1	Samaria	G6
Bowmont	F2	Fernwood	B2	Lewisville	F6	Samuels	A2
Brownlee Dam	E2	Filer	G4	Liberty	G7	Sanders	B2
Brownlee Reservoir	E1	Firth	F6	Lincoln	F6	Sandpoint	A2
Bruneau	G3	Fish Haven	G7	Little Wood River	F4	Santa	B2
Bruneau River	G3	Fort Hall	F6	Lochsa River	C3	Sawtooth Mountains	E3
Buhl	G4	Fort Hall Indian Reservation	G6	Lolo Pass	C4	Sawtooth National Recreation Area	E3
Burke	B3	Franklin	G7	Lookout Pass	B3	Selkirk Mountains	A2
Burley	G5	Fruitland	F2	Lorenzo	F7	Selway River	C3
Cabinet Mountains	A2	Fruitvale	E2	Lost River	F5	Seven Devils Mountains	D2
Calder	B2	Garden City	F2	Lost River Range	E4	Shelley	F6
Caldwell	F2	Garden Valley	E3	Lowman	E3	Shoshone	G4
Cambridge	E2	Genesee	C2	Lucile	D2	Shoshone Falls	G4
Carey	F5	Georgetown	G7	Mackay	F5	Silverton	B3
Careywood	A2	Gibbonsville	D5	Magic Reservoir	F4	Smelterville	B2
Caribou Range	F7	Gifford	C2	Malad City	G6	Smiths Ferry	E2
Carmen	D5	Glenns Ferry	G3	Malta	G5	Smoky Mountains	F4
Cascade	E2	Gooding	G4	Marsing	F2	Snake River	E1
Cascade Reservoir	E3	Goose Creek	G5	Marysville	G6	Snake River Plain	F6
Castleford	G4	Grace	G7	May	E5	Snake River Range	F7
Cavendish	C2	Grand View	G2	McCall	E2	Soda Springs	G7
Centennial Mountains	E6	Grangeville	D2	McCammon	G6	Southwick	C2
Center Mountains	D3	Grays Lake	F7	Meadow Creek	A2	Spalding	C2
Challis	E4	Greencreek	C2	Meadows	E2	Spencer	E6
Chatcolet	B2	Greer	C2	Melba	F2	Spirit Lake	B2
Chester	F7	Hagerman	G4	Menan	F7	Springfield	F6
Chubbuck	G6	Hailey	F4	Meridian	F2	St. Anthony	F7
Clark Fork	A2	Hamer	F6	Mesa	E2	St. Charles	G7
Clarkia	C2	Hammett	G3	Midas	A2	St. Joe River	B3
Clayton	E4	Hansen	G4	Middleton	F2	St. Maries	B2
Clearwater	C3	Harrison	B2	Midvale	E2	Stanley	E4
Clearwater Mountains	C2	Harvard	C2	Minidoka	G5	Star	F2
Clearwater River	C2	Hauser Lake	B2	Minidoka Dam	G5	Sterling	F6
Clifton	G7	Hayden	B2	Minkcreek	G7	Stites	C3
Cobalt	D4	Hayden Lake	B2	Monteview	F6	Stone	G6
Cocolalla	A2	Hazelton	G4	Montour	F2	Sublett Range	G6
Coeur d'Alene	B2	Headquarters	C3	Montpelier	G7	Sugar City	F7
				Moore	F5	Sun Valley	F4
				Moreland	F6	Swan Falls	F2
				Moscow	C2	Swan Valley	F7
				Mount Idaho	D2	Swanlake	G6
				Mountain Home	F3	Sweet	F2
				Moyle Springs	A2	Targhee Pass	E7
				Mud Lake	F6	Tendoy	E5
				Mullan	B3	Tensed	B2
				Murphy	F2	Terreton	F6
				Murray	B3	Teton	F7
				Murtaugh	G4	Tetonia	F7
				Nampa	F2	Thatcher	G7
				Naples	A2	Thornton	F7
				New Meadows	D2	Troy	C2
				New Plymouth	F2	Tuttle	G4
				Newdale	F7	Twin Falls	G4
				Nez Perce Indian Reservation	C2	Ucon	F7
				Nezperce	C2	Victor	F7
				North Fork	D5	Viola	C1
				North Loon Mountains	D3	Walcott Lake	G5
				Notus	F2	Wallace	B3
				Oakley	G5	Wardner	B2
				Ola	E2	Warren	D3
				Old Town	A1	Wasatch Range	G7
				Onaway	C2	Weippe	C3
				Orchard	F2	Weiser	E2
				Orofino	C2	Weiser River	E2
				Osburn	B3	Wendell	G4
				Ovid	G7	Weston	G7
				Owyhee Mountains	G2	White Bird	D2
				Owyhee River	G2	White Knob Mountains	F5
				Oxford	G6	Wilder	F2
				Palisades	F7	Winchester	C2
				Palisades Reservoir	F7	Woodville	F6
				Paris	G7	Worley	B2
				Parker	F7	Yellow Jacket Mountains	D4

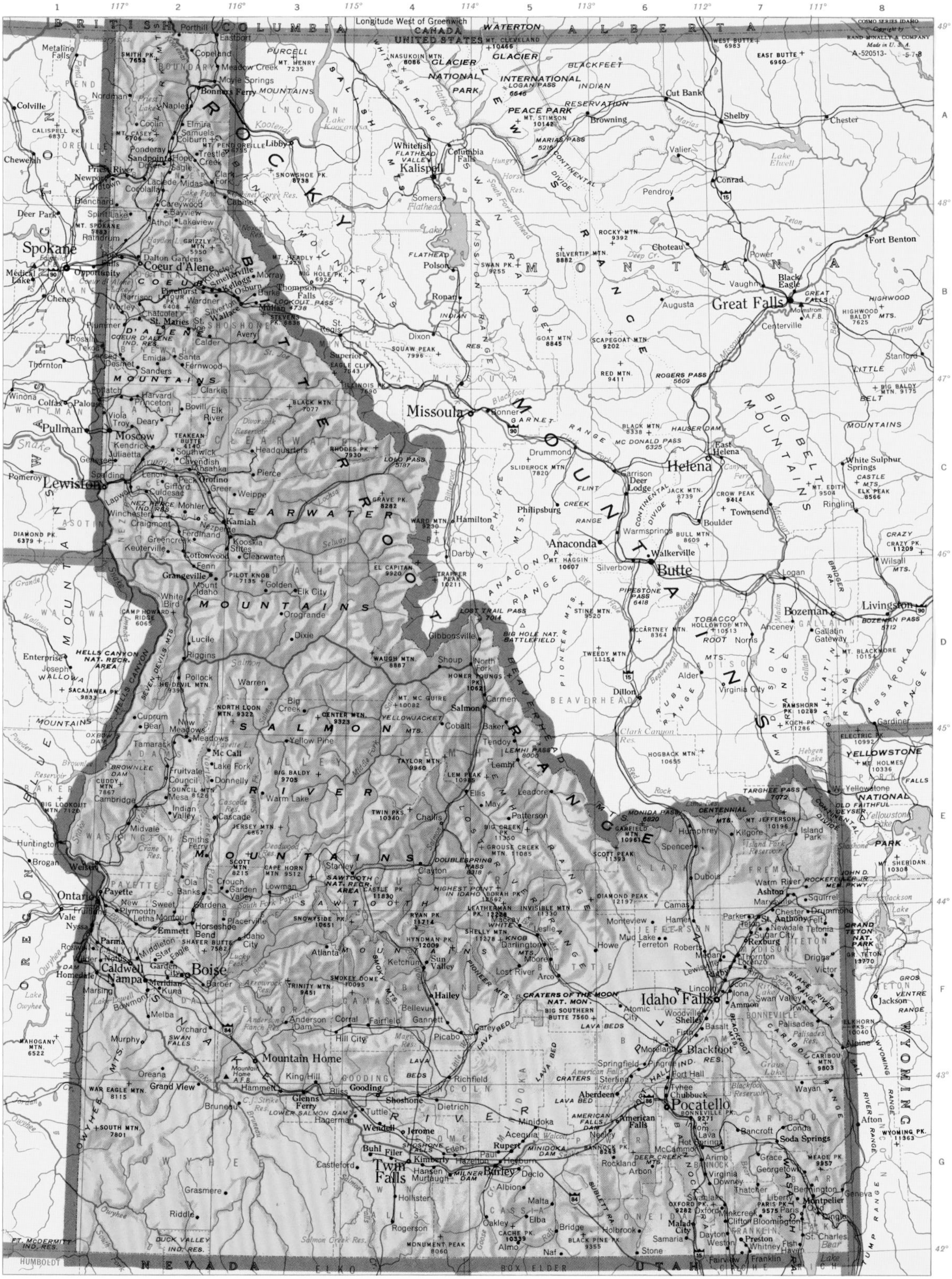

COSMO SERIES IDAHO
RAND McNALLY & COMPANY
Made in U.S.A.
A-520513-
S-7-8

Longitude West of Greenwich

BRITISH COLUMBIA — **CANADA** — **ALBERTA**
UNITED STATES

MONTANA

WYOMING

NEVADA — **UTAH**

Spokane
Coeur d'Alene
Lewiston
Moscow
Pullman
Missoula
Helena
Butte
Great Falls
Bozeman
Livingston
Boise
Nampa
Caldwell
Mountain Home
Twin Falls
Pocatello
Idaho Falls
Ontario

ROCKY MOUNTAINS
BITTERROOT
CLEARWATER MOUNTAINS
SALMON RIVER MOUNTAINS
SAWTOOTH MOUNTAINS
BEAVERHEAD RANGE
LOST RIVER RANGE

GLACIER NATIONAL PARK
YELLOWSTONE NATIONAL PARK
GRAND TETON NAT. PARK
CRATERS OF THE MOON NAT. MON.
HELLS CANYON NAT. RECR. AREA

POTATOES   BEEF

FOREST PRODUCTS   POULTRY

DAIRY PRODUCTS   MINING

MANUFACTURING   WHEAT

SUGAR BEETS   HAY

VEGETABLES   FRUIT

BARLEY   SHEEP

HOGS   BEANS

OATS

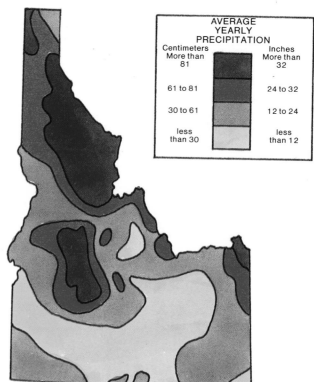

AVERAGE YEARLY PRECIPITATION

Centimeters		Inches
More than 81		More than 32
61 to 81		24 to 32
30 to 61		12 to 24
less than 30		less than 12

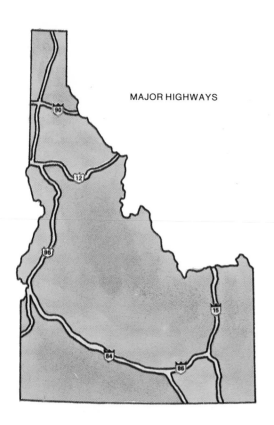

MAJOR HIGHWAYS

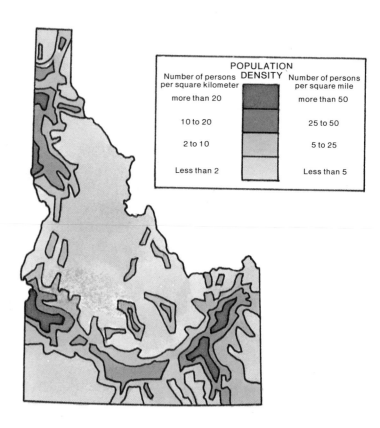

POPULATION DENSITY

Number of persons per square kilometer		Number of persons per square mile
more than 20		more than 50
10 to 20		25 to 50
2 to 10		5 to 25
Less than 2		Less than 5

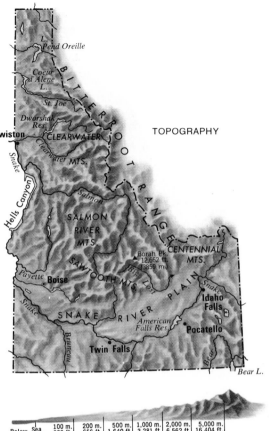

TOPOGRAPHY

Borah Pk.
12,662 ft.
(3859 m.)

Courtesy of Hammond, Incorporated
Maplewood, New Jersey

Below	Sea Level	100 m. 328 ft.	200 m. 656 ft.	500 m. 1,640 ft.	1,000 m. 3,281 ft.	2,000 m. 6,562 ft.	5,000 m. 16,404 ft.

COUNTIES

A ranch near New Meadows

INDEX

Page numbers that appear in boldface type indicate illustrations

The Salmon River, known for its furious rapids, is sometimes called the "River of No Return."

Picture Identifications

Front Cover: Stanley Lake and the Sawtooth Range
Back Cover: Middle fork of the Boise River, Boise National Forest
Pages 2-3: Dent Bridge over Dworshak Reservoir in northern Idaho
Page 6: Big Southern Butte as seen from the Lost River Range
Pages 8-9: Farmland in the Bruneau Valley
Page 20: Montage of Idaho residents
Page 26: Ancient Indian petroglyphs along the Snake River
Pages 40-41: A turn-of-the-century photograph of a Nez Perce ceremonial dance
Page 52: Farmland in northern Idaho
Page 68: The Idaho State Capitol in Boise
Pages 80-81: Rafting on the Payette River
Pages 90-91: Hells Canyon of the Snake River
Page 108: Montage showing the state tree (western white pine), the state flag, the state bird
(mountain bluebird), and the state flower (syringa)

Picture Acknowledgments

Front cover, © D. Muench/**H. Armstrong Roberts**; 2-3, 4, 5, 6, © **John Marshall**; 8-9, © Ed Cooper; 11, 12 (two photos), © **John Marshall**; 13, © **Ed Cooper**; 15 (two photos), 17 (two photos), © **John Marshall**; 18 (left), © **Jerry Hennen**; 18 (right), © Carl R. Sams, II/**M.L. Dembinsky Jr. Photography Assoc.**; 19, © **John Marshall**; 20 (top left), © Sally A. Beyer/**Root Resources**; 20 (top middle), © **David R. Frazier Photolibrary**; 20 (top right, bottom left), © **John Marshall**; 20 (bottom right), © Robert Frerck/**Odyssey Prod.**; 23, © **John Marshall**; 24, © **David R. Frazier Photolibrary**; 26, 28, © **John Marshall**; 30 (top left, bottom left), **North Wind Picture Archives**; 30 (right), **Historical Pictures Service, Chicago**; 33, **North Wind Picture Archives**; 34, **Historical Pictures Service, Chicago**; 35 (left), © **David R. Frazier Photolibrary**; 35 (right), © **Ed Cooper**; 36, **Idaho State Historical Society**; 37, © **Ed Cooper**; 39, © **Jeff Greenberg**; 40-41, **Idaho State Historical Society**; 43, **North Wind Picture Archives**; 44 (left), **Historical Pictures Service, Chicago**; 44 (right), **North Wind Picture Archives**; 47, **Idaho State Historical Society**; 48, **Courtesy of John Clymer estate**; 51, © **Jeff Greenberg**; 52, © **John Marshall**; 56, 58, **Idaho State Historical Society**; 60, © **John Marshall**; 62, © **David R. Frazier Photolibrary**; 64, © **John Marshall**; 65, **UPI/Bettmann Newsphotos**; 67, 68, © **John Marshall**; 71 (left), © **David R. Frazier Photolibrary**; 71 (right), © **Ed Cooper**; 72, © **Joan Dunlop**; 74 (left), © **John Marshall**; 74 (right), © **Buddy Mays**; 75, © **John Marshall**; 76 (left), © **David R. Frazier Photolibrary**; 76 (right), © **John Marshall**; 77, © **David R. Frazier Photolibrary**; 78, © **John Marshall**; 79, © **David R. Frazier Photolibrary**; 80-81, © **Buddy Mays**; 83 (two pictures), **Historical Pictures Service, Chicago**; 85, © Doug Wilson/**The Marilyn Gartman Agency**; 86 (two photos), © **David R. Frazier Photolibrary**; 88, © Gary Brettnacher/**Shostal/SuperStock**; 89, 90-91, 93, © **John Marshall**; 93 (map), **Len W. Meents**; 94 (left), © **John Marshall**; 94 (right), © Mark E. Gibson/**The Marilyn Gartman Agency**; 96, © **John Marshall**; 96 (map), **Len W. Meents**; 97, © **Buddy Mays**; 99, © **John Marshall**; 99 (map), **Len W. Meents**; 100 (left), © **John Marshall**; 100 (right), © **David R. Frazier Photolibrary**; 101, 102 (left), © **Ed Cooper**; 102 (right), 104, © **John Marshall**; 104 (map), **Len W. Meents**; 105 (left), © D. Muench/**H. Armstrong Roberts**; 105 (right), 106, 107, © **John Marshall**; 108 (tree), © Kohout Productions/**Root Resources**; 108 (flag), **Courtesy Flag Research Center, Winchester, Massachusetts 01890**; 108 (bird), © **Jerry Hennen**; 108 (flowers), © **David R. Frazier Photolibrary**; 112, © **Ed Cooper**; 113, © Robert Frerck/**Odyssey Prod.**; 114 (left), © Sally A. Beyer/**Root Resources**; 114 (right), © **David R. Frazier Photolibrary**; 115 © **Lynn M. Stone**; 116, © **David R. Frazier Photolibrary**; 117 © Doug Wilson/**The Marilyn Gartman Agency**; 119 (left), © **Buddy Mays**; 119 (right), © Robert Frerck/**Odyssey Prod.**; 121, © Mark E. Gibson/**The Marilyn Gartman Agency**; 122, © **John Marshall**; 123, © Robert Frerck/**Odyssey Prod.**; 124, © David Stoecklein/**Root Resources**; 126 (two photos), **Idaho State Historical Society**; 127, © **John Marshall**; 128 (Alexander), **Idaho State Historical Society**; 128 (Borglum), **Historical Pictures Service, Chicago**; 128 (Bridger), **North Wind Picture Archives**; 129 (Church), **UPI/Bettmann Newsphotos**; 129 (Farnsworth), **AP/Wide World Photos**; 129 (Fisher, Harriman), **Historical Pictures Service, Chicago**; 129 (Hawley, Lewis), **North Wind Picture Archives**; 130 (Johnson), **AP/Wide World Photos**; 130 (Joseph), © **Smithsonian Institution**; 131 (Orchard), **North Wind Picture Archives**; 131 (Pfost), **Historical Pictures Service, Chicago**; 131 (Pound), **AP/Wide World Photos**; 131 (Smylie), **UPI/Bettmann Newsphotos**; 132 (Steunenberg), **Idaho State Historical Society**; 132 (Turner), **Historical Pictures Service, Chicago**; 136 (maps), **Len W. Meents**; 138, 141, back cover, © **John Marshall**

About the Author

Zachary Kent grew up in Little Falls, New Jersey. He is a graduate of St. Lawrence University and holds a teaching certificate in English. After college, he worked for two years at a New York City literary agency before launching his writing career. He is the author of many of books of American history and biography for young people.